Let My PEOPLE GO

Let My PEOPLE GO

JANNIE M. WILCOXSON

© 2006 by Jannie M. Wilcoxson. All rights reserved.

WinePress Publishing (PO Box 428, Enumclaw, WA 98022) functions only as book publisher. As such, the ultimate design, content, editorial accuracy, and views expressed or implied in this work are those of the author.

No part of this publication may be reproduced, stored in a retrieval system or transmitted in any way by any means—electronic, mechanical, photocopy, recording or otherwise—without the prior permission of the copyright holder, except as provided by USA copyright law.

Unless otherwise noted, all Scriptures are taken from the New American Standard Bible, © 1960, 1963, 1968, 1971, 1972, 1973, 1975, 1977, 1995 by The Lockman Foundation. Used by permission.

Scripture references marked KJV are taken from the King James Version of the Bible.

ISBN 1-57921-868-7
Library of Congress Catalog Card Number: 2006904565

Printed in Colombia.

Table of Contents

Who Bewitched You?
    Chapter 1: The Chains   11
    Chapter 2: Bondage? What? When? Me?   17
    Chapter 3: Know Who You Are   25

Responses to Bondage
    Chapter 4: An Individual's Response   33
    Chapter 5: Boot Camp   39
    Chapter 6: A Nation's Response   43

Who's Influencing Whom?
    Chapter 7: Bondage: Blinding and Binding   51
    Chapter 8: Others' Trouble Troubling You   57
    Chapter 9: Rebellious Leaders, Rebellious People   61
    Chapter 10: The Devil Made Me…   65

Who's to Blame?
    Chapter 11: Whom Will God Hold Accountable?   77
    Chapter 12: The Last Sermon   83

Recognizing the Bondages
    Chapter 13: Self-inflicted: Recognize It!   91
    Chapter 14: From Others: Check It!   99
    Chapter 15: Under the Circumstances: Watch It!   107
    Chapter 16: Freedom's Cloak: Wear It!   115

Jesus' Assignment: "Break the Yoke"
    Chapter 17: Shepherds and Sheep   123
    Chapter 18: Freedom Promised   127
    Chapter 19: What He Did   131
    Chapter 20: The Bondage—Broken   137

Your Assignment: "Take the Yoke"
    Chapter 21: So What's the Problem?   145
    Chapter 22: They Had It But Didn't Get It   153
    Chapter 23: A Made-up Mind   157

Why God Allows It
    Chapter 24: Purpose Planned   163
    Chapter 25: Potential Perfected   171

Living in the Freedom of Christ
    Chapter 26: You'd Better Know It!   181
    Chapter 27: Pleasing Him   187
    Chapter 28: Keep It Clean   197

Depending on the Guidance of the Spirit
    Chapter 29: Spiritual Mind-set   209
    Chapter 30: Why God Promised His Spirit   215
    Chapter 31: Interceding in the Deep   223

Relying on the Word of God
    Chapter 32: Let the Word Dwell Richly   231
    Chapter 33: Freedom Assured   241
    Chapter 34: High Rate of Return   245

Promises to the Obedient and the Disobedient
    Chapter 35: Standing on the Promises or Hanging around the Premises   255
    Chapter 36: My Presence Will Go with You   261
    Chapter 37: Promises Guaranteed   273

Appendix   283
Bibliography   297

Who Bewitched You?

Chapter One

THE CHAINS

Bondage abounds! Everywhere people are in chains, in prison, in a battle for the soul. Whether the bondage is physical, mental, emotional, intellectual, psychological, moral, or spiritual, manipulation is always behind this fight for control. Some people know they are being held captive and want to be set free. Others know but think they cannot be free. Still others don't even want to be free. Some don't know; some can't tell; some think it's normal, and some simply don't care.

The world is filled with people who are angry, discouraged, hurt, bitter, lonely, depressed, dejected, defeated, and self-absorbed. Our society is filled with broken relationships. We are rich yet poor, well fed but starving, laughing but crying. People are in bondage to their own lusts, brainwashed by their poor self-images, enemies of their own souls.

People who have been battered in the name of love are now perishing for the want of love. Without love, a man, woman, boy, or girl only exists; with love they live. You know the verse: "For God so loved the world, that He gave His only begotten Son, that whoever believes in Him shall not perish, but have eternal life" (John 3:16). There is only one place you can find the true love that lasts. It is in God, through Christ Jesus.

Church buildings are in every city, every state, every country, almost on every corner, some occupied by several different groups. But the church is just as much in bondage as the world.

If we are doing everything that God is calling us to do, why have our problems multiplied? If we are so blessed, why are we so stressed? If we are so anointed, why are we so disappointed?

Is There a Difference?

Do our religious beliefs actually affect the way we behave? In 1997, the Barna Group conducted a nationwide survey measuring the attitudes, behaviors, values, and beliefs of one thousand or more adult Christians and non-Christians.[1] The study covered lifestyle aspects such as TV viewing, donating to nonprofit organizations, taking illegal drugs or prescription medications for depression, buying lottery tickets, marriage and divorce, encouraging others, and sending letters to companies protesting their ethics.

Surprisingly, this study found no noticeable differences between the two groups. The Christians (those who stated that they have confessed their sinfulness and have asked Jesus Christ to be their Lord and Savior) seem to have fallen prey to the same thoughts and behaviors as their worldly counterparts.

The study also showed that fewer than 10 percent of American Christians possess a biblical worldview, looking at life through the filter of the Bible. Most Christians make important decisions on the basis of instinct, emotion, past experience, assumptions, external pressure, or chance. Very few are involved in the disciplines necessary to integrate scriptural truth into daily life.

In addition, conclusions based on a series of nationwide surveys, each conducted among one thousand or more adults, completed from 1994 to 1996, indicated that in a typical week, about half of all adults listen to preaching or Bible teaching, one third read the Bible, one out of ten study the Scriptures, and less than one out of twenty-five memorize even one Bible verse. Less than 2 percent are committed to all four practices on a weekly basis.

In other words, most Christians do not live in a way that is quantifiably different from non-Christians, in spite of the fact that they profess to believe in a set of principles that should clearly set them apart.

Can you see why there are so many bondages, problems, and issues that Christians do not know how to handle? It's because there is no consistent spiritual growth. Many do not know truth, cannot identify truth, are not loyal to God, and have no absolutes, but are merely doing what is right in their own eyes. God has set the standard. Only His Word, His truth, will make you free. God's message is this: ***"Let My people go."***

---

[1] See "The American Witness" The Barna Report, November/December 1997.

The Chains

The Same Old Problem

What is happening in the Christian community today is not new. Paul was amazed that the people in Galatia, to whom he had preached the gospel of Jesus Christ, were deserting the gospel for another. They were troubled by some who were preaching contrary to the truth of the gospel of Jesus, seeking to exchange works for grace (Galatians 1:6–7). The false teachers were demanding that the Christians (Jews and Gentiles) be circumcised. And they were saying that people would be righteous before God if they observed the Jewish law to the letter (Galatians 2–5).

Paul was concerned for the believers, as well as those who had made a superficial profession, because the truth was being distorted. He addressed the bondage from two positions. (1) Salvation: Christ sets a person free from bondage to sin and the law. (2) Sanctification: God provides freedom from sin's control and bondage to all those who live lives of faith and righteousness.

As it was then, so it is now. Those who subtly distort the true gospel of Jesus Christ by diluting, maligning, or otherwise twisting Scripture are bigger enemies of the church than those who openly contradict the Word of God.

Understanding the Scriptures

How important is it to understand the Bible? Is it even possible? Can you really know what is true and what is false? Is there a way to tell when truth is being taught from the Bible and when the Word of God is being twisted, whether intentionally or unintentionally? Is man really left to his own opinions, traditions, and human philosophies? Is everyone supposed to have his own interpretation of the Bible? Does it really make sense that God would leave people to pool their ignorance, telling one another what they don't know about His Word?

If this is true, then Christianity is meaningless and the Bible has no message for us. If an individual can make the Bible say what he wants it to say, the Bible cannot guide him. It simply becomes a tool to support his own ideas. The good news is that the Bible was not written with that purpose in mind.

If the Bible is truly God's Word, revealing His will, nothing could be more important than understanding it. If it was given to reveal the truth, God must intend that we understand it. If we don't understand it, the fault lies with us, not with Him.

Second Timothy 3:16 says, "All scripture is inspired by God and profitable for" the following four things:

(1) Doctrine: teaching, principles of wisdom, or divine truth
(2) Reproof: showing us what is wrong
(3) Correction: showing the correct way
(4) Instruction in righteousness: "This is the way; walk in it."

The Bible is sufficient in and of itself. It can take someone who does not know God, who is not saved, and make him wise unto salvation. Then it will teach him, reprove him when he does wrong, point out the right thing to do, and show him how to walk in the right path.

The result in the next verse (17) is "so that the man of God may be adequate, equipped for every good work."

What about Truth?

We live in a world filled with people searching for truth. They read, study, reason, listen, talk, and interact, but they never get the real truth. "…always learning and never able to come to the knowledge of the truth" (2 Timothy 3:7).

How can truth be identified? In John 17:17 Jesus, praying to the Father, says, "Your word is truth." In John 14:6 Jesus says, ""I am the way, and the truth, and the life." Listen to what Jesus says about Himself and the Word in John 8:31–32." If you continue in My word, then you are truly disciples of Mine; and you will know the truth, and the truth will make you free."

Man will grope and search and struggle for truth until he finds it, and when he does he will be free. If you want real truth, study the Bible for yourself. In it you will find the truth about God and man; life and death; sin and forgiveness; heaven and hell; love and hate; families, married couples, and singles; friends and enemies; leaders and followers; work, home, community, government, and church; even the truth about how you ought to eat and drink, what to say, and what to think. The truth is all there, and it brings joy when you obey it.

Many people know what the Bible says but they forfeit freedom and joy because they refuse to obey it. If you are tired of the struggle and deception and you really want to know truth, and the freedom and joy that accompany obedience to truth, it is available to you in—the Word of God.

You Can Be Free

If you want to be free, read the Word. Study the Word. We cannot function on what we don't know. We cannot apply a truth we haven't discovered. We cannot operate on a principle we never knew. The Psalmist said, "Thy word have I hid in mine heart, that I might not sin against thee" (Psalm 119:11 KJV).

As we read and study the Word, it becomes the resource by which the Holy Spirit directs and guides us. When you know the Word and use it, you will be victorious over the world, Satan, and the flesh.

Will you be caught up in the deception, captured in the bondage? Or will you live in the freedom that God in Christ provides? Will you be the victim or the victor? Will you triumph in Christ and be a sweet aroma of the knowledge of Him? Will you accept and receive all that God has to offer?

The Chains

As you read the verses below, contemplate what is before you. Notice who gives the victory and who always leads us in triumph in Christ. Record your answers.

But thanks be to God, who gives us the victory through our Lord Jesus Christ.
—1 Corinthians 15:57

Who gives the victory?

But thanks be to God, who always leads us in triumph in Christ, and manifests through us the sweet aroma of the knowledge of Him in every place.
—2 Corinthians 2:14

Who always leads us to triumph in Christ?
What is the result?

Spend time thanking God for Jesus, for victory in every situation, and for what He has made available to you through the Savior.

Chapter Two
─────────────

BONDAGE? WHAT? WHEN? ME?

To be in bondage is to be enslaved by another person, a habit, or and an attitude; to be dependent upon; to be deprived of freedom. It could be physical, mental, emotional, psychological, moral, intellectual, or spiritual entrapment. It could be external or internal pressure, self-inflicted or inflicted by others.

A few years ago I met a woman who told me she had been ensnared by several different bondages. She was trapped, unhappy, and full of turmoil, almost to the point of hopelessness, unfulfilled and seeking relief. She says:

I can remember being sexually molested by my uncle. It started when I was six. This led to feeling as if I had no self-worth and my body meant nothing. It was only a thing to be used. This led to sexual promiscuity and thinking that in order to have love and to be accepted, I had to give my body to someone, anyone. That led to the abuse of drugs and alcohol and even suicidal tendencies. Then rape entered the picture, along with being deeply hurt by several boyfriends, and that led to a distrust of men, which led to inordinate affection for women.
Finally, I turned to God to save and direct me. I began to internalize that I did not have to be in bondage and that my freedom and deliverance had already been provided for. I know that obedience to God's Word is the key to victory over bondage, and by relying on my Lord completely, I can be released from any form of bondage that the enemy would send my way.

Victory! She found the solution in Jesus. So many others could, but do not.

The Pain of Bondage

Your wounds, pain, and hurt may be unbearable. Bruises, both internal and external, have left scars and pain. You could be feeling dirty, used, or abused. Any abnormal use of a person—whether sexual, physical, mental, emotional, verbal, spiritual, financial, or psychological—can cause pain. The pain may have been self-inflicted or inflicted by someone else. It may have occurred last year, last month, or last night.

The memories of the past sometimes push their way into the present. Yesterday flows into today, and pain is rehearsed over and over. Wounds that are picked at, left unattended, or poorly attended will fester and fill with pus. The poison will seep into the soul and overflow into all parts of your life. Feelings of never being good enough, thoughts of worthlessness or hopelessness, or the inability to cope sometimes overwhelm us and result in useless activity, depression, oppression, and sadness.

Is this pain meant to last forever? What is the solution? Suicide is too permanent and doesn't solve anything. Killing the other person will put you into prison. Drugs, alcohol, and illicit sex may be temporary forms of escape, but the price tags of addiction, guilt, and fear are far too costly.

Whether you believe it or not, you are beloved of God, He desires complete healing and wholeness for you. Your sorrow is not beyond healing. There really is a balm in Gilead (Jeremiah 8:22). God has a miraculous system of deliverance that is activated when you trust Him. If you have been trying to solve your problem or looking for someone else to solve it, forget it. You can't; they can't. But God can.

Read the following Scriptures to determine where or from whom bondages may come, what holds a person in bondage, how it is initiated, and the solution. Circle the word *bondage,* underline *God* and *Jesus* and record your findings. (Study Tip: If you will make a distinctive mark [i.e., circle, underline, square, or color] in the passage you are studying, including applicable pronouns, it will increase your retention and make it easier to spot answers.)

For I see that you are in the gall of bitterness and in the bondage of iniquity.

—Acts 8:23

What do you see about bondage?

For the wrath of God is revealed from heaven against all ungodliness and unrighteousness of men who suppress the truth in unrighteousness.

—Romans 1:18

Bondage? What? When? Me?

Why are these men in bondage?

Or do you not know that the unrighteous will not inherit the kingdom of God? Do not be deceived; neither fornicators, nor idolaters, nor adulterers, nor effeminate, nor homosexuals, nor thieves, nor the covetous, nor drunkards, nor revilers, nor swindlers, will inherit the kingdom of God. Such were some of you; but you were washed, but you were sanctified, but you were justified in the name of the Lord Jesus Christ and in the Spirit of our God.
—1 Corinthians 6:9–11

When Paul writes to the church at Corinth, he reminds them of what they used to be. If they had remained in these bondages of sin, according to the passage above, what would they not partake of?

How have Jesus and the Spirit changed their lives?

But it was because of the false brethren secretly brought in, who had sneaked in to spy out our liberty which we have in Christ Jesus, in order to bring us into bondage.
—Galatians 2:4

Where was their freedom?

Who was trying to lead them into bondage?

> But now that you have come to know God, or rather to be known by God, how is it that you turn back again to the weak and worthless elemental things, to which you desire to be enslaved all over again?
>
> —Galatians 4:9

Can you think of any reason a person would want to be enslaved?

> See to it that no one takes you captive through philosophy and empty deception, according to the tradition of men, according to the elementary principles of the world, rather than according to Christ.
>
> —Colossians 2:8

What was the responsibility of the person toward bondage?

> The Lord's bond-servant must not be quarrelsome, but be kind to all, able to teach, patient when wronged, with gentleness correcting those who are in opposition, if perhaps God may grant them repentance leading to the knowledge of the truth, and they may come to their senses and escape from the snare of the devil, having been held captive by him to do his will.
>
> —2 Timothy 2:24–26

Who is holding the people captive?

How is it that God may grant repentance?

Bondage? What? When? Me?

What could repentance lead to?

What must God's bondservant do?

And with whom was He angry for forty years? Was it not with those who sinned, whose bodies fell in the wilderness? And to whom did He swear that they would not enter His rest, but to those who were disobedient? So we see that they were not able to enter because of unbelief.
—Hebrews 3:17–19

What is the bondage?

List two reasons that kept them from entering.

So many ways to be in bondage! And the list could go on. Whether it is suppressing the truth, false teachers, erroneous teaching, bitterness, sin, the snare of the devil, previous lifestyles, philosophy, traditions of men, unbelief, or any other areas, it all goes back to not believing in God and not living in His truth. It happens to believers and unbelievers alike.

The Real Solution

There is something wrong when we go into church and come out the same way we went in, week in and week out (or should we say, "weak in and weak out?"). Singing to one another, preaching to one another, ushering one another around, with no real change in the lives of the people. People trying to get delivered from something Christ has already delivered them from

(Colossians 2:13–14). Some returning to get delivered from the same sin, the same habit, the same attitude, or the same bondage they thought they were delivered from last week.

How many more will die who should still be alive? How many will remain weak when they should be strong? How many will be sick when God sent His word to heal? The folks in 1 Corinthians 11 were Christians who did not or would not properly discern the Lord's body. It is amazing how we can accept Christ for salvation but will not go to Him for all He desires us to have. It's bondage when we become so satisfied and so comfortable that we cannot move to where God would have us to be, ultimately rejecting the abundant life God wants for all His children.

God's people have been set free! If you are not living in freedom, you are cheating yourself or allowing someone else to cheat you out of all God has for you. His message is: ***Let My People Go!***

God has provided a solution in the person of Jesus Christ, who came to set the captives free (Isaiah 61:1). Freedom not only for salvation, but from now until Jesus comes. He has provided His Spirit, for "where the Spirit of the Lord is, there is liberty" (2 Corinthians 3:17).

He has also provided His Word. Jesus said, "You will know the truth, and the truth will make you free" (John 8:32).

Second Chronicles 20:6 says that power and might are in God's hand and no one can stand against Him. Jeremiah 29:11 says, "I know the plans that I have for you." God's sole intent is to give you a future and a hope. You can't do it, but God can!

Don't play the "what if?" game…"What if the situation changes? What if this person leaves? What if the money doesn't come in time?" What if…what if…what if. "If" may never happen! And if it does, it doesn't really matter. So release your grip. Submit to God. Trust Him.

God promises in 2 Corinthians 12:9, "My grace is sufficient for you, for power is perfected in weakness." So you can rest in the sovereignty of God. He is in control, and His solution is always best. When you trust Him, you can have the assurance that God will fulfill His purpose for you and perfect that which concerns you. You can't, but God can!

Everyone is influenced by his or her own past and present, but none who trust God have to be controlled by either. The bondage-breaking process happens when you trust God and become conformed by the renewing of your mind. When the new comes in, the old is tossed out. Whatever situation you are in, Jesus wants to set you free to live in His ways. Remember, "and you will know the truth, and the truth will make you free" (John 8:32). You can't, but God can.

Job 14:1 says, "Man that is born of a woman is of few days, and full of trouble" (KJV). We have trouble during this life. But we have God's promises to get us through.

Underline and write out Jesus' promises, instruction, and exhortation in the following Scripture:

Bondage? What? When? Me?

> These things I have spoken to you, so that in Me you may have peace. In the world you have tribulation, but take courage; I have overcome the world.
>
> —John 16:33

The promises:

The instruction:

The exhortation:

Rejoice in the Lord and write out a prayer of praise, thanking God for Jesus, who has overcome the world.

Chapter Three

KNOW WHO YOU ARE

Where are the ones who know the truth and have been set free? Where are the ones like Jude who wanted to write about our common salvation, but wrote instead to beg the saints to earnestly contend for the faith that had been handed to them? Where are the ones who are set free enough to warn the saints that savage wolves will come in among them, not sparing the flock, and that some will arise right in their midst to draw away the disciples? Will anyone sound the warning about those who will come in sheep's clothing, twisting the Word of God, sometimes in words, more often by actions, promising freedom when they themselves are slaves of corruption? God said it before and the message is the same today: ***"Let My people go."***

Making an Impact

You say you know truth and you are set free? Then the question becomes, "Do you know who you are in the freedom that God in Christ has made available to you? And are you making an impact in the world today?"

Does anyone know we are here? We are saved, chosen, called out, the elect, the *elklesia*, a royal priesthood, a holy nation, a peculiar people, but does anyone recognize it in us? We are overcomers by the blood of the Lamb, more than conquerors and seated in heavenly places with Christ, but does a dying world see a living Savior in us? We are sanctified, justified, and called to be saints, but does our practice reflect our position? Christ enriches us in everything, and everything is ours because we belong to Christ and He to God, but do these riches show up in our homes, in the marketplace, on our jobs, in the community, or even in our churches?

Does the world see us as examples of Christ? Do they desire to glorify God when they see our good works? To glorify God means to give a correct opinion of Him (make Him look good). Are we making Him look bad because others cannot see Him in us on a consistent basis? Have we forgotten that we are not our own, that we have been bought with a price (the blood of Jesus)? Have we gotten caught up in the day-to-day routine and neglected to serve God with our whole heart, soul, mind, and spirit?

Have we so conformed to the world that we do what the world does and say what the world says? There are as many believers (or so-called believers) as there are unbelievers in the courts, in the lottery lines, buying X-rated movies, at the dog races, on the gambling boats, taking drugs for depression, involved in division and strife, immorality, living together as if married, just doing whatever seems right in their own eyes.

We have the mind of Christ, but instead we use our own wisdom to make decisions. What a shame to have the mind of Christ and not use it as He intended.

How will we ever tell a dying world about a living Savior when we live like we are not sure who we are and whose we are? Oh, we know all the right words and a lot of the Scripture verses. We even know the names of God. We know He is Jehovah Rapha, but we neglect the Word He sent to heal us. We know He is the living bread, but we refuse to dine at His table. We call Him El Shaddai, but refuse to believe He is our all-sufficient God.

We want Him to order our steps in His Word, but are not interested in attending Sunday school or Bible study. We know His Word is a lamp unto our feet and a light unto our paths, but we keep walking according to our own plans. We know that God hears and answers prayer, and we are angry about legislation against prayer in the schools, yet we seem to forget that we can pray at home and in our hearts. We know He is our protection, but we keep looking to other things for protection, whether a person, a weapon, an alarm system, a job, money, whatever. We know the Word will send our enemies running, even the devil himself, but we fight the battle ourselves anyway.

We say we know the Word, but we are running, struggling, falling, fainting, undeveloped, and ill equipped to live victoriously in order to show the world Jesus. That, my friend, is bondage! If we are not ravenously feeding on the Word, we will be anemic in our nourishment, stunted in our growth, overly dependent on others, and too vulnerable to wrong teaching to help anyone. God's message is: ***"Let My People Go!"***

Developing Your Walk

Read the following Scriptures, mark the word *walk,* and record how believers are to walk and not walk.

Know Who You Are

Therefore I, the prisoner of the Lord, implore you to walk in a manner worthy of the calling with which you have been called, with all humility and gentleness, with patience, showing tolerance for one another in love, being diligent to preserve the unity of the Spirit in the bond of peace.

—Ephesians 4:1–3

How are believers to walk?

How are believers not to walk?

WORD STUDY

The Greek word for "walk" is *peripateo*, meaning "to tread all around; i.e., walk at large (especially as proof of ability); figuratively, to live, deport oneself, follow (as a companion or votary), go, be occupied with, walk about."

According to the definition above, what does it mean to walk?

Since believers have been called to salvation, our lives are to be directly proportionate to all that we have received in the salvation package. As you read, mark *walk* and *truth*.

So this I say, and affirm together with the Lord, that you walk no longer just as the Gentiles also walk, in the futility of their mind, being darkened in their understanding, excluded from the life of God because of the ignorance that is in them, because of the hardness of their heart; and they, having become callous, have given themselves over to sensuality for the practice of every kind of impurity with greediness. But you did not learn Christ in this way, if indeed you have heard Him and have been taught in Him, just as truth is in Jesus, that, in reference to your former manner of life, you lay aside the old self, which is being corrupted in accordance with

the lusts of deceit, and that you be renewed in the spirit of your mind, and put on the new self, which in the likeness of God has been created in righteousness and holiness of the truth.
—Ephesians 4:17–24

How is the believer to walk?

Do you see anything the believer is not to do?

Therefore do not be partakers with them; for you were formerly darkness, but now you are Light in the Lord; walk as children of Light (for the fruit of the Light consists in all goodness and righteousness and truth), trying to learn what is pleasing to the Lord.
—Ephesians 5:7–10

How is the believer to walk?

Therefore be careful how you walk, not as unwise men but as wise, making the most of your time, because the days are evil. So then do not be foolish, but understand what the will of the Lord is. And do not get drunk with wine, for that is dissipation, but be filled with the Spirit.
—Ephesians 5:15–18

How is the believer to walk?

Does your walk line up with what you have read in Ephesians? Can others see it? Is society experiencing the impact of your Ephesian walk? All believers have the ability in God to live free, to rise above any bondage situation.

If we are not walking so that the world sees Jesus, what shall we do? Shall we continue in sin that grace may abound, as Romans 6:1–2 asks? May it never be! Since the Spirit of God dwells in us to guide us, lead us, teach us, and empower us to do all that God has called us to do, and since we don't live godly lives in our own power, God is always at work in us both to will and to work for His good pleasure (Philippians 2:13).

Since He has given us a hunger and a thirst for His Word and the supernatural ability to live holy, and since our steps are already ordered by God, won't He provide for His own? Isn't His eye in every place and His ear open to our cry? Hasn't He promised to perfect that which concerns us and not to ever leave us? Indeed He has.

Jesus is on His way back, and our assignment is almost over. So let's yield to the Spirit of God consistently. Now is the time to move, to walk, and to live so that someone knows God is in you. The world needs to see a living Savior in us, alive and well on a daily basis.

Not sure how to walk consistently so the world can see God in you and so God can be glorified? Confess and repent of any sin you may be aware of. Then write out a prayer of commitment to your Father.

Responses to Bondage

Chapter Four

An Individual's Response

When God called Abram out of Ur of the Chaldees, He promised him descendants, land, and to make him a great nation (Genesis 12). In Genesis 15:6 we read that Abram believed God for righteousness. God made a covenant with him and his descendants forever. He also promised that they would be in captivity for four hundred years in a land that was not theirs.

Just as God promised, Abram became the father of Isaac, and Isaac became the father of Jacob, and Jacob the father of twelve sons. The sons of Jacob were jealous of Joseph, their brother, and sold him into slavery. (Note that this was bondage for the brothers and for Joseph.) But God rescued Joseph from all his afflictions and granted him favor and wisdom in the sight of Pharaoh, king of Egypt, and he became governor over Egypt thirteen years later.

Let's look at Joseph's response in a couple of situations while he was in bondage. Remember, God ordained and designed the bondage, but He also provided a way of escape so that Joseph could bear it. Mark *Lord*, and *Joseph*.

> Now Joseph had been taken down to Egypt; and Potiphar, an Egyptian officer of Pharaoh, the captain of the bodyguard, bought him from the Ishmaelites, who had taken him down there. The Lord was with Joseph, so he became a successful man. And he was in the house of his master, the Egyptian. Now his master saw that the Lord was with him and how the Lord caused all that he did to prosper in his hand. So Joseph found favor in his sight and became his personal servant; and he made him overseer over his house, and all that he owned he put in his

charge. It came about that from the time he made him overseer in his house and over all that he owned, the Lord blessed the Egyptian's house on account of Joseph; thus the Lord's blessing was upon all that he owned, in the house and in the field. So he left everything he owned in Joseph's charge; and with him there he did not concern himself with anything except the food which he ate. Now Joseph was handsome in form and appearance.

—Genesis 39:1–6

How is Joseph described? What is the Lord doing while Joseph is in bondage? How is Joseph's relationship with God described? What is happening to Potiphar? Record your findings.

Mark *God, Joseph* and pronouns pertaining to Joseph.

It came about after these events that his master's wife looked with desire at Joseph, and she said, "Lie with me." But he refused and said to his master's wife, "Behold, with me here, my master does not concern himself with anything in the house, and he has put all that he owns in my charge. "There is no one greater in this house than I, and he has withheld nothing from me except you, because you are his wife. How then could I do this great evil and sin against God?" As she spoke to Joseph day after day, he did not listen to her to lie beside her or be with her.

—Genesis 39:7–23

Potiphar's wife makes a simple request of a good-looking man. What is her request and what is Joseph's response?

How many times does she make the request? (Who is really in bondage here?) What is Joseph's response?

An Individual's Response

Read on, marking *Lord, Joseph* (and pronouns), *jail* and *prosper:*

Now it happened one day that he went into the house to do his work, and none of the men of the household was there inside. She caught him by his garment, saying, "Lie with me!" And he left his garment in her hand and fled, and went outside. When she saw that he had left his garment in her hand and had fled outside, she called to the men of her household and said to them, "See, he has brought in a Hebrew to us to make sport of us; he came in to me to lie with me, and I screamed. When he heard that I raised my voice and screamed, he left his garment beside me and fled and went outside." So she left his garment beside her until his master came home. Then she spoke to him with these words, "The Hebrew slave, whom you brought to us, came in to me to make sport of me; and as I raised my voice and screamed, he left his garment beside me and fled outside." Now when his master heard the words of his wife, which she spoke to him, saying, "This is what your slave did to me," his anger burned. So Joseph's master took him and put him into the jail, the place where the king's prisoners were confined; and he was there in the jail. But the Lord was with Joseph and extended kindness to him, and gave him favor in the sight of the chief jailer. The chief jailer committed to Joseph's charge all the prisoners who were in the jail; so that whatever was done there, he was responsible for it. The chief jailer did not supervise anything under Joseph's charge because the Lord was with him; and whatever he did, the Lord made to prosper.

—Genesis 39:11–23

When Potiphar's wife is rejected, she responds in anger and Joseph is sent to prison. He is already in bondage, in captivity in Egypt. Now he is in prison, in real bondage. Or is he? How does Joseph respond? What does the Lord do? Record your findings.

Potiphar's wife continues to seduce Joseph daily, actually grabbing him and trying to force herself on him. Would you call this bondage? For the sake of satisfying the flesh, this married woman seems to give no thought to her spouse and the sanctity of marriage. Can you see a similar pattern around us today?

A Look at Marriages Today

What has satisfying the flesh done in the marriages of today? What has happened to marriage the way God intended? Why are so many marriages either on the rocks or headed for them? Why are so many divorcing, why are so many living together without the benefit of wedding vows? Why are so many being unfaithful in marriage? Why so much lying, cheating, lack of trust, and disrespect among spouses? Why the selfishness, pride, materialism, laziness, and loneliness, even among those who decide to remain married? Is marriage becoming a thing of the past?

What happened to the couple who said, "For richer or poorer, for better or worse, in sickness and health, I will love, honor, and cherish you, till death do us part?" They joined hands, exchanged rings, and said, "I do." They made a promise and were pronounced man and wife. They kissed each other, ran down the aisle while rice was being thrown, then sped away together to live happily ever after. But was there real commitment?

To commit is to turn something over to someone. It is to yield, to surrender, to entrust, to place at the disposal of another. In a marriage, two people are committing to turn themselves over to each another, to yield, to surrender totally to each other and to no one else, even to the point of denying themselves, until death parts them. If there was real commitment in marriage, divorce courts would not have a single case.

The world's a mess, which doesn't surprise us. But the sad truth is that this has crept into the church as well. Christians and non-Christians alike are having marital problems. The answer is not another book on marriage, or another conference, workshop, or seminar on marriage. It is not more counselors or another tape. We must simply go back to God's original plan and design for marriage.

The Bible says that marriage is honorable, and the marriage bed is to undefiled. (Hebrews 13:4) That means no sex outside of marriage.

> To avoid pre-marital sex, get married.
> A man is to have his own wife.
> A woman is to have her own husband
> Wives have authority over their husbands' bodies.
> Husbands have authority over their wives' bodies. (1 Corinthians 7:1–5)
> Wives, submit to your husbands.
> Husbands, love your wives.
> Wives, respect your husbands. (Ephesians 5:22–33)
> Husbands, live with your wife in an understanding way; honoring her as a fellow heir of grace
> so your prayers will be answered. (1 Peter 3:7)

Can you have a meaningful relationship apart from knowing God? Sure, but only to a certain extent. Since God created the institution of marriage and family, in order for it to work the way God intended, you must follow the Creator's original design. Then watch the blessings follow your obedience!

Whether you have been married for three years or thirty or longer, whether you are planning a wedding ceremony or you're in what appears to be a hopeless situation, you can have a right relationship, where you can be all God intended for you to be. When you follow the Creator's

An Individual's Response

design, marriage can be everything God made it to be, creating a harmonious union that fulfills every need of the human heart.

Did you see a connection between obedience and favor, prosperity, or blessings? If so, what is the connection? (Think back to Joseph for a moment, physically captured, yet free to obey God.) Regardless of your situation, you too can experience His favor and enjoy His blessings.

Meditate on the following Scripture and record your insights.

> This book of the law shall not depart from your mouth, but you shall meditate on it day and night, so that you may be careful to do according to all that is written in it; for then you will make your way prosperous, and then you will have success.
>
> —Joshua 1:8

Do you really want His blessings? Are you willing to be obedient in every situation? Whatever your circumstances, God gives beauty for ashes, gladness for mourning, a mantle of praise for a spirit of fainting. You will be called an oak of righteousness, the planting of the Lord, that He may be glorified. (See Isaiah 61:3.)

Don't let disobedience cheat you out of your blessing. Write out a prayer to God, thanking Him for your circumstances and for your blessings in the midst of them.

Chapter Five

BOOT CAMP

Joseph moves from one situation to another, but God has orchestrated every one. This young man goes from the pasture (watching the flock) to the pit (when his brothers throw him in) to Potiphar's house, to prison, and finally to the palace. All those years, God had Joseph in training for his palace assignment.

God even used the prison experience to move Joseph to the palace. There Joseph became known as an interpreter of dreams, so when Pharaoh had a dream, Joseph was brought from prison to interpret it. He warned the king of a famine in the land and explained how the country could survive with proper management of their resources. Pharaoh liked Joseph's ideas and put him over all the land of Egypt. Mark *God* as you read.

> Now before the year of famine came, two sons were born to Joseph, whom Asenath, the daughter of Potiphera priest of On, bore to him. Joseph named the firstborn Manasseh, "For," he said, "God has made me forget all my trouble and all my father's household." He named the second Ephraim, "For," he said, "God has made me fruitful in the land of my affliction."
> —Genesis 41:50–52

Record what Joseph says about the meanings of his sons' names.

Manasseh:

Ephraim:

The famine spread throughout the land of Canaan and Egypt, and there was great affliction. Joseph's brothers could find no food. But Jacob, their father, heard there was grain in Egypt so he sent them to buy grain. They had to make their request of their brother Joseph, whom they did not recognize. On their second visit, Joseph made himself known to his brothers, weeping with such intensity that even the household of Pharaoh heard it. He forgave them and invited them to bring the entire family to live in Egypt with him. Look at what Joseph said to them that time. Mark *God* and *Joseph*.

> Then Joseph said to his brothers, "Please come closer to me." And they came closer. And he said, "I am your brother Joseph, whom you sold into Egypt. Now do not be grieved or angry with yourselves, because you sold me here, for God sent me before you to preserve life. For the famine has been in the land these two years, and there are still five years in which there will be neither plowing nor harvesting. God sent me before you to preserve for you a remnant in the earth, and to keep you alive by a great deliverance. Now, therefore, it was not you who sent me here, but God; and He has made me a father to Pharaoh and lord of all his household and ruler over all the land of Egypt."
>
> —Genesis 45:4–8

Record Joseph's response to his brothers' actions toward him. If you read carefully you will see God's purpose. Record it.

After their father dies, the brothers are still a little uncertain about Joseph's forgiveness of them. Mark *God* and *Joseph*.

Boot Camp

When Joseph's brothers saw that their father was dead, they said, "What if Joseph bears a grudge against us and pays us back in full for all the wrong which we did to him!" So they sent a message to Joseph, saying, "Your father charged before he died, saying, 'Thus you shall say to Joseph, "Please forgive, I beg you, the transgression of your brothers and their sin, for they did you wrong."' And now, please forgive the transgression of the servants of the God of your father." And Joseph wept when they spoke to him. Then his brothers also came and fell down before him and said, "Behold, we are your servants." But Joseph said to them, "Do not be afraid, for am I in God's place? As for you, you meant evil against me, but God meant it for good in order to bring about this present result, to preserve many people alive. So therefore, do not be afraid; I will provide for you and your little ones." So he comforted them and spoke kindly to them.

—Genesis 50:15–21

What did Joseph's brothers think he would do? Joseph had been in captivity in Egypt for thirteen years. Does it appear that the brothers were also in captivity? Could they have been in bondage to their sin all these years? Record Joseph's response.

Did you see him release them from their bondage? What would have happened if they had found no food? God used Joseph to preserve a nation.

God had made a covenant with Abraham. He promised him descendants. He promised to make him a great nation. He promised that all the nations of the earth would be blessed through Abraham. God stood on His promise by preserving a nation.

SELAH…Think about it.

Would you have responded as Joseph did if you were in a situation like his, through no fault of your own?

Are you in God's boot camp? Are you on His training ground?

Is there someone you can release from bondage today?

Is God using your present situation for His future glory?

Spend some time in prayer, asking God to show you His purpose for your life.

Chapter Six

A Nation's Response

The Israelites had been in Egypt for about four hundred years. God had promised Abraham that they would be released, and it was almost time. Joseph had died, along with all his brothers and that generation. There was a new king over Egypt, one who did not know Joseph, but he was very aware of the people of Israel. They had grown from the seventy who came out of Canaan into Egypt to more than 600,000 men, plus the women and children.

The king thought they were too many and too mighty, and they kept multiplying. Afraid of what would happen in the event of war, Pharaoh appointed taskmasters to afflict them with hard, rigorous labor that made their lives bitter. He even instructed the midwives to put to death all the male babies as the women were giving birth and to throw them into the Nile.

Unknown to the king, God was accomplishing His purpose. The midwives feared God and did not kill the babies.

At this time Moses was born, and he was nurtured for three months in his father's home. Finally, when she could hide him no longer, Moses' mother put him in a basket and placed it on the Nile. God intervened.

Pharaoh's daughter saw him floating in the river and took him as her own. The woman she hired to nurse him was his own mother, who came highly recommended by a little girl named Miriam (Moses' sister). Isn't it just like God to bring the man He will use to deliver His people right to the man who gave the order to kill him?

Moses was educated, and he grew up to be a man of power in words and deeds. At about the age of forty, he killed an Egyptian, trying to defend an Israelite who was being oppressed. (Wrong way to get someone out of bondage). He thought the Israelites would understand that God was granting them deliverance through him, but they didn't. On the contrary, they confronted him about the Egyptian he had killed asking "who made you ruler and judge over us" (Acts 7:27).

Moses, afraid the king knew of the matter, ran from the presence of Pharaoh and settled in Midian, where he married and had two sons. Forty years later an angel of the Lord appeared to him in a burning bush and gave him an assignment.

Read the following Scriptures; record how the people respond and what God does. Mark *God, covenant, oppression* and *bondage.*

> Now it came about in the course of those many days that the king of Egypt died. And the sons of Israel sighed because of the bondage, and they cried out; and their cry for help because of their bondage rose up to God. So God heard their groaning; and God remembered His covenant with Abraham, Isaac, and Jacob. God saw the sons of Israel, and God took notice of them.
> —Exodus 2:23–25

> The Lord said, "I have surely seen the affliction of My people who are in Egypt, and have given heed to their cry because of their taskmasters, for I am aware of their sufferings. So I have come down to deliver them from the power of the Egyptians, and to bring them up from that land to a good and spacious land, to a land flowing with milk and honey, to the place of the Canaanite and the Hittite and the Amorite and the Perizzite and the Hivite and the Jebusite. Now, behold, the cry of the sons of Israel has come to Me; furthermore, I have seen the oppression with which the Egyptians are oppressing them."
> —Exodus 3:7–9

Describe the people and God's response.

Moses' assignment was to go to Egypt, lead the people out, and tell Pharaoh from God, ***"Let My people go."*** Moses didn't seem too shocked by the assignment, but he didn't believe he was the man for the job. Forty years ago, sure, but not today!

A Nation's Response

God assured Moses that He would bring the people out. He told him what to say to convince the people. He also told him what to say to convince the king. He even warned him that the king would not let the people go except under compulsion. This was not going to be easy!

Moses pleaded with God about his speaking abilities, seeming to forget all about his Egyptian training, not to mention his household management and flock pasturing training. (If you recall, Joseph had some of that same training.) God assigned Aaron, Moses' brother, to help. In the meantime the people were still in bondage.

Read Exodus 4:29–31 and record the response of the people when they realized God had sent a deliverer to get them out of bondage. Mark *Lord, Moses,* and *people.*

> Then Moses and Aaron went and assembled all the elders of the sons of Israel; and Aaron spoke all the words which the Lord had spoken to Moses. He then performed the signs in the sight of the people. So the people believed; and when they heard that the Lord was concerned about the sons of Israel and that He had seen their affliction, then they bowed low and worshiped.
> —Exodus 4:29–31

Moses and Aaron go to Pharaoh to give him God's message: ***"Let My people go."*** The king refused, saying he did not even know the Lord. He accused Moses of drawing the people away from their work. That day he instructed the taskmasters to change the work standard. The workload became heavier. The straw used for brick making, which was previously provided for them, was cut off. They had to get the material wherever they could find it, while their daily brick-making quotas remained the same. Pharaoh's instruction was, "Let the labor be heavier on the men, and let them work at it, so that they will pay no attention to false words" (Exodus 5:9). They were called lazy and they were beaten. The people tried to plead with the king, but their efforts were useless.

Read Exodus 5:19–23 and record the response of the foreman of the sons of Israel. Also record Moses' specific request of the Lord. Mark *Moses* and *Lord.*

> The foremen of the sons of Israel saw that they were in trouble because they were told, "You must not reduce your daily amount of bricks." When they left Pharaoh's presence, they met Moses and Aaron as they were waiting for them. They said to them, "May the Lord look upon you and judge you, for you have made us odious in Pharaoh's sight and in the sight of his servants, to put a sword in their hand to kill us." Then Moses returned to the Lord and said, "O Lord, why have You brought harm to this people? Why did You ever send me? Ever since

I came to Pharaoh to speak in Your name, he has done harm to this people, and You have not delivered Your people at all."

—Exodus 5:19–23

Now read Exodus 6:2–9 marking *God, covenant, bondage* and *know*.

God spoke further to Moses and said to him, "I am the Lord; and I appeared to Abraham, Isaac, and Jacob, as God Almighty, but by My name, Lord, I did not make Myself known to them. "I also established My covenant with them, to give them the land of Canaan, the land in which they sojourned. Furthermore I have heard the groaning of the sons of Israel, because the Egyptians are holding them in bondage, and I have remembered My covenant. Say, therefore, to the sons of Israel, 'I am the Lord, and I will bring you out from under the burdens of the Egyptians, and I will deliver you from their bondage. I will also redeem you with an outstretched arm and with great judgments. Then I will take you for My people, and I will be your God; and you shall know that I am the Lord your God, who brought you out from under the burdens of the Egyptians. I will bring you to the land which I swore to give to Abraham, Isaac, and Jacob, and I will give it to you for a possession; I am the Lord.'" So Moses spoke thus to the sons of Israel, but they did not listen to Moses on account of their despondency and cruel bondage.

—Exodus 6:2–9

What is God's promise? What will the people know after God brings them out from under the burdens of the Egyptians? Why won't they listen?

God wants everyone to know that He is God, and He will use His people to get the message out. In Exodus 7:5, to whom will He make Himself known, and how will He do it?

The Egyptians shall know that I am the Lord, when I stretch out My hand on Egypt and bring out the sons of Israel from their midst.

—Exodus 7:5

A Nation's Response

Pharaoh was headed for deep water when he decided to trouble the Israelites by afflicting them with hard labor. He did not know God. God would get His people out, but not before showing Pharaoh who He was.

God struck the land with ten plagues. After the tenth plague, in which the king's own firstborn son died, he finally decided to let the people go. But he changed his mind as the 600,000+ non-paid workforce walked out.

Pharaoh knew who God was. He knew enough about Him to request prayer through Moses. He admitted he was a sinner and that God was righteous. He saw God making a distinction between the Israelites and the Egyptians. The king's servants and magicians had recognized the finger of God and requested the release of the people.

In the end, the Egyptians drowned in the Red Sea, the Israelites were set free, and everyone knew who God was!

God used the plagues to get the attention of Pharaoh, the Egyptians, and the Israelites. Does God have your attention? Do you know Him? Will you believe Him? Don't let bondage keep you from hearing God.

Could God be using you to show people who He is? Will you respond so they will know Him? Use the space below to record what is on your heart.

Who's Influencing Whom?

Chapter Seven

BONDAGE: BLINDING AND BINDING

Some people are in bondage and don't even know it. They have eyes but cannot see, ears but cannot hear (Isaiah 43:8). As you examine these Scriptures notice the blinding, binding, and other captivating effects that bondage has on its victims, both body and soul. Underline those who are in bondage.

Now the two angels came to Sodom in the evening as Lot was sitting in the gate of Sodom. When Lot saw them, he rose to meet them and bowed down with his face to the ground. And he said, "Now behold, my lords, please turn aside into your servant's house, and spend the night, and wash your feet; then you may rise early and go on your way." They said however, "No, but we shall spend the night in the square." Yet he urged them strongly, so they turned aside to him and entered his house; and he prepared a feast for them, and baked unleavened bread, and they ate. Before they lay down, the men of the city, the men of Sodom, surrounded the house, both young and old, all the people from every quarter; and they called to Lot and said to him, "Where are the men who came to you tonight? Bring them out to us that we may have relations with them." But Lot went out to them at the doorway, and shut the door behind him, and said, "Please, my brothers, do not act wickedly. "Now behold, I have two daughters who have not had relations with man; please let me bring them out to you, and do to them whatever you like; only do nothing to these men, inasmuch as they have come under the shelter of my roof." But they said, "Stand aside." Furthermore, they said, "This one came in as an alien, and already he is acting like a judge; now we will treat you worse than them." So they pressed hard against Lot and came near to break the door. But the men reached out their hands and brought Lot into the house with them, and shut the door. They struck the men who were at the doorway of the house with blindness, both small and great, so that they wearied themselves trying to find the doorway. Then the two men said to Lot, "Whom else have you here? A son-in-law, and your sons, and your daughters, and whomever you have in the city, bring them out of the place."

—Genesis 19:1–12

List those who are in bondage and to what they are in bondage. How do they respond?

"We are about to destroy this place, because their outcry has become so great before the Lord that the Lord has sent us to destroy it." Lot went out and spoke to his sons-in-law, who were to marry his daughters, and said, "Up, get out of this place, for the Lord will destroy the city." But he appeared to his sons-in-law to be jesting. When morning dawned, the angels urged Lot, saying, "Up, take your wife and your two daughters who are here, or you will be swept away in the punishment of the city." But he hesitated. So the men seized his hand and the hand of his wife and the hands of his two daughters, for the compassion of the Lord was upon him; and they brought him out, and put him outside the city. When they had brought them outside, one said, "Escape for your life! Do not look behind you, and do not stay anywhere in the valley; escape to the mountains, or you will be swept away." But Lot said to them, "Oh no, my lords! "Now behold, your servant has found favor in your sight, and you have magnified your loving-kindness, which you have shown me by saving my life; but I cannot escape to the mountains, for the disaster will overtake me and I will die; now behold, this town is near enough to flee to, and it is small. Please, let me escape there (is it not small?) that my life may be saved." He said to him, "Behold, I grant you this request also, not to overthrow the town of which you have spoken. "Hurry, escape there, for I cannot do anything until you arrive there." Therefore the name of the town was called Zoar.

—Genesis 19:13–22

Add to your list of who is in bondage. Record the response of each.

Bondage: Blinding and Binding

When Lot hesitates what do you see about the Lord?

Lot was the nephew of Abram (Genesis 12:5) who set out with him from Haran to the land of Canaan. They went to Egypt together to avoid a famine that was in Canaan. Returning from Egypt, they had so many possessions they could not live together. Their herdsmen could not get along, so to avoid further strife, Abram offered Lot an option.

> So Abram said to Lot, "Please let there be no strife between you and me, nor between my herdsmen and your herdsmen, for we are brothers. "Is not the whole land before you? Please separate from me; if to the left, then I will go to the right; or if to the right, then I will go to the left." Lot lifted up his eyes and saw all the valley of the Jordan, that it was well watered everywhere—this was before the Lord destroyed Sodom and Gomorrah—like the garden of the Lord, like the land of Egypt as you go to Zoar. So Lot chose for himself all the valley of the Jordan, and Lot journeyed eastward. Thus they separated from each other. Abram settled in the land of Canaan, while Lot settled in the cities of the valley, and moved his tents as far as Sodom. Now the men of Sodom were wicked exceedingly and sinners against the Lord.
> —Genesis 13:8–13

Record Abram's offer and Lot's choice. Also record all you see about Sodom.

In Genesis 14 the king of Sodom is in a war along with eight other kings. Lot is still living in Sodom.

> Then they took all the goods of Sodom and Gomorrah and all their food supply, and departed. They also took Lot, Abram's nephew, and his possessions and departed, for he was living in Sodom. Then a fugitive came and told Abram the Hebrew. Now he was living by the oaks of Mamre the Amorite, brother of Eshcol and brother of Aner, and these were allies with Abram. When Abram heard that his relative had been taken captive, he led out his trained men, born in his house, three hundred and eighteen, and went in pursuit as far as Dan. He divided his forces against them by night, he and his servants, and defeated them, and pursued them as far

as Hobah, which is north of Damascus. He brought back all the goods, and also brought back his relative Lot with his possessions, and also the women, and the people.

—Genesis 14:11–16

Record all you see about Lot.

Who rescues Lot from captivity?

How much is restored?

The New Testament passage below refers back to the Sodom and Gomorrah account. How is Lot described? How did the conduct of others affect him? What was happening to his soul?

If He condemned the cities of Sodom and Gomorrah to destruction by reducing them to ashes, having made them an example to those who would live ungodly lives thereafter; and if He rescued righteous Lot, oppressed by the sensual conduct of unprincipled men (for by what he saw and heard that righteous man, while living among them, felt his righteous soul tormented day after day by their lawless deeds), then the Lord knows how to rescue the godly from temptation, and to keep the unrighteous under punishment for the day of judgment.

—2 Peter 2:6–9

From what was Lot rescued? What do you learn about God's response to the godly and to the unrighteous? What confidence can you put in God's rescue techniques?

Bondage: Blinding and Binding

Read the following verse. Underline *God* and make a list of everything you see about Him. What do you see about those being tempted?

> No temptation has overtaken you but such as is common to man; and God is faithful, who will not allow you to be tempted beyond what you are able, but with the temptation will provide the way of escape also, so that you will be able to endure it.
> —1 Corinthians 10:13

Have you noticed how easy it is to recognize when another person is in bondage? Often we can come up with a solution, a Scripture, or words of encouragement for them. We can see the far-reaching effects in their lives, in their families, in the people around them, in their bodies, and even the impact on their soul and spirit. Yet we often miss it when we are in bondage ourselves.

Is there a situation you need to wake up to, get out of or rise above? Has God provided a way of escape yet you are still holding out? Do you understand when it is time to go or time to stay? Do you know when not to go at all?

What part do you play in your freedom? Does attitude have anything to do with it? What role does God play in your freedom?

Answer the above questions and spend some time talking to God about situations that you may be blind to. Ask Him to show you what to do. He has the answers. God wants you to be free. He has a plan for your life. Walk in it!

Chapter Eight

OTHERS' TROUBLE TROUBLING YOU

Some people are in bondage because they are listening to others and not to God. Those others may not know truth but speak as if they do. The standard is the Word of God and nothing else. If deception is to be recognized and truth is to be known, we must know God and His Word.

Read 2 Timothy 3:1–9, underline and make a list of how the last days are described and what the people will be like. Circle *men, women* and *truth*.

> But realize this, that in the last days difficult times will come. For men will be lovers of self, lovers of money, boastful, arrogant, revilers, disobedient to parents, ungrateful, unholy, unloving, irreconcilable, malicious gossips, without self-control, brutal, haters of good, treacherous, reckless, conceited, lovers of pleasure rather than lovers of God, holding to a form of godliness, although they have denied its power; Avoid such men as these. For among them are those who enter into households and captivate weak women weighed down with sins, led on by various impulses, always learning and never able to come to the knowledge of the truth. Just as Jannes and Jambres opposed Moses, so these men also oppose the truth, men of depraved mind, rejected in regard to the faith. But they will not make further progress; for their folly will be obvious to all, just as Jannes' and Jambres' folly was also.
> —2 Timothy 3:1–9

These men love themselves, hate good, are unholy, and do not love God. You can already see the bondage they are in. Although they deny God's power, what do they have a form of?

We are told in the passage above to avoid these religious men. What is their relationship to the women? Describe the women. What is the relationship of the women to truth?

If the women are always learning, why can't they come to the knowledge of truth?

What is the relationship of the men to truth?

After reading the description of what people will be like in the last days, why are so many drawn to them? Externally they look good. They act godly, as if they belong to God, like some leaders in the Christian community today. They have made their way into homes, whether through the door, the TV, radio, video, tapes, books, CDs, or word of mouth. These are in bondage, capturing by deception others who are already in bondage. Although many are taken captive, sin will not be broken and complete deliverance will never come because they have denied the power of God and therefore have no power available to them to break sin or to obtain complete deliverance.

WORD STUDY

The Greek word for "captive" is *aichmaloteuo*, which means "to take captive by deception."

Others' Trouble Troubling You

The externals may be grand but their lifestyles do not subdue sin and nurture holiness. Be discerning. This is not a rare group. These are folks you will run into constantly in these last days.

Read 2 Timothy 4:3–5. Notice what time it is! Look at the response of the people to the bondage. Make a list of what the people want. From what will they turn and to what will they turn? Circle *truth*.

> For the time will come when they will not endure sound doctrine; but wanting to have their ears tickled, they will accumulate for themselves teachers in accordance to their own desires, and will turn away their ears from the truth and will turn aside to myths. But you, be sober in all things, endure hardship, do the work of an evangelist, fulfill your ministry.
> —2 Timothy 4:3–5

Read Titus 1:10–16. How are these men described? Who are they upsetting? From what do they turn? Circle *truth;* mark *God* (and applicable pronouns).

> For there are many rebellious men, empty talkers and deceivers, especially those of the circumcision, who must be silenced because they are upsetting whole families, teaching things they should not teach for the sake of sordid gain. One of themselves, a prophet of their own, said, "Cretans are always liars, evil beasts, lazy gluttons." This testimony is true. For this reason reprove them severely so that they may be sound in the faith, not paying attention to Jewish myths and commandments of men who turn away from the truth. To the pure, all things are pure; but to those who are defiled and unbelieving, nothing is pure, but both their mind and their conscience are defiled. They profess to know God, but by their deeds they deny Him, being detestable and disobedient and worthless for any good deed.
> — Titus 1:10–16

The deceivers have the ear of the people, they are very deceptive, and they do what they do for money. They have infiltrated the homes and they are influencing and impacting whole families. Remember, we are not talking about those outside the Christian community, not the drug dealers, prostitutes, murderers, or thieves on the streets, not white-collar or blue-collar criminals in business and industry. We are talking about those in the Christian community who are not godly, but hold to a form of godliness. They are teaching things they do not know and should not teach, just for money or status. In their greed, they are buying and selling people with their twisted words, enticing by fleshly desires, enslaved to corruption themselves, yet trying to tell others how to be free.

Why do we give more generously when the appeal is glossy and stylish? We listen more intently when the voice is famous, familiar, or well known. Just because you see it does not mean that God is in it. What is personally beneficial to you should not be put above solid biblical truth. Deception comes in many forms, both open and subtle. So be careful. Don't be fooled by the size, the gloss, the style, or the latest fad. Be aware of following the crowd and compromising doctrine, even when the crowd is a religious one.

Reread Titus 1:10–16. Describe what you see in that Scripture passage. Do these people know God? What do you see about their minds and their consciences? How do they deny Him? Can you see the form of godliness? Can you see the absence of holiness?

If you are having difficulty consistently seeing everything as God sees, ask Him to help you see as He does. Ask God to help you look at everything through the eyes of Scripture, to be aware and discerning. Ask Him to help you know the difference between truth and error and to make direct application in your life so others can see Him in you and glorify Him. Take time to do that right now.

Chapter Nine

REBELLIOUS LEADERS, REBELLIOUS PEOPLE

Read Isaiah 30. Mark *Lord, people,* and *listen.*

"Woe to the rebellious children," declares the Lord, "Who execute a plan, but not Mine, And make an alliance, but not of My Spirit, In order to add sin to sin…" "Everyone will be ashamed because of a people who cannot profit them, Who are not for help or profit, but for shame and also for reproach." The oracle concerning the beasts of the Negev. Through a land of distress and anguish, From where come lioness and lion, viper and flying serpent, They carry their riches on the backs of young donkeys And their treasures on camels' humps, To a people who cannot profit them; Even Egypt, whose help is vain and empty. Therefore, I have called her "Rahab who has been exterminated." Now go, write it on a tablet before them And inscribe it on a scroll, That it may serve in the time to come As a witness forever. For this is a rebellious people, false sons, Sons who refuse to listen To the instruction of the Lord; Who say to the seers, "You must not see visions"; And to the prophets, "You must not prophesy to us what is right, Speak to us pleasant words, Prophesy illusions. "Get out of the way, turn aside from the path, Let us hear no more about the Holy One of Israel."

—Isaiah 30:1, 5–11

Record how the people are identified.

Read the verses again. Rebellious leaders begat rebellious people. Describe their response in this bondage of rebellion. What do they want to hear, and what do they not want to hear?

12 Therefore thus says the Holy One of Israel, "Since you have rejected this word and have put your trust in oppression and guile, and have relied on them, therefore this iniquity will be to you like a breach about to fall, a bulge in a high wall, whose collapse comes suddenly in an instant, whose collapse is like the smashing of a potter's jar, so ruthlessly shattered that a sherd will not be found among its pieces to take fire from a hearth or to scoop water from a cistern."
—Isaiah 30:12–14

What do they reject? What do they put their trust in and rely on?

WORD STUDY

The Hebrew word for "trust" in verse 12 is *batach*, which means "to attach oneself, trust, confide in, feel safe, be secure." The Hebrew word for "oppression" is *osheq*, meaning "a thing deceitfully gotten, oppression by means of fraud or extortion."

In their rebellion, they rejected the word, but trusted in oppression. They attached themselves to that which was fraudulent and deceitful, something they thought would fulfill their needs and make them feel safe and secure.

Be careful of attaching yourself to someone or something that pulls you away from dependency on God. Some have put their trust in money, jobs, other people, homes, ministries, and even church, either in addition to or instead of God. When we trust in something or someone other than God, we fall short of God's blessings, training ourselves in ungodliness.

Rebellious Leaders, Rebellious People

Reread Isaiah 30:12–14 above and record God's judgment.

For thus the Lord GOD, the Holy One of Israel, has said, "In repentance and rest you will be saved, In quietness and trust is your strength." But you were not willing, And you said, "No, for we will flee on horses," Therefore you shall flee! "And we will ride on swift horses," Therefore those who pursue you shall be swift. One thousand will flee at the threat of one man; You will flee at the threat of five, Until you are left as a flag on a mountain top And as a signal on a hill. Therefore the Lord longs to be gracious to you, And therefore He waits on high to have compassion on you. For the Lord is a God of justice; How blessed are all those who long for Him.
—Isaiah 30:15–18

According to the passage, how can they be saved, and where is their strength? What is their response?

WORD STUDY

The Hebrew word for "salvation" is *Yasha,* meaning "to be open, wide, or free." When you have plenty of room in which to move, you feel safe and secure. Repenting and resting in Him and in His truth will give you plenty of room to be safe and secure.

What does God want to do for the people and where is the blessing?

They were not willing. Remember the folks in 2 Timothy who had a form of godliness but were deceiving and being deceived, who opposed truth, wanting their teachers to teach only what they wanted to hear? And the ones in Titus who were deceivers, rebellious, and turned away from truth, who professed to know God but denied Him? The people in Isaiah 30 who were rebellious and refused to listen to the truth had the same problem.

Read Isaiah 29:13. Besides being rebellious and deceived, and turning away from truth, what else do they have in common with those in Titus and Timothy?

> Then the Lord said, "Because this people draw near with their words and honor Me with their lip service, but they remove their hearts far from Me, and their reverence for Me consists of tradition learned by rote."
>
> —Isaiah 29:13

God's call to Holiness

God's call is for holiness and a lifestyle of obedience. He is looking for people who will live the way He designed them to live, walking worthy of the call. Not just those who will say, "Hallelujah," or, "Glory to God," or, "I love You, Lord," but who will do exploits that display His strength. Not just those who show up once a week for church or even midweek for Bible study and prayer meeting, but those who live so others can see Him.

God is looking for honor and reverence from His people. In the gospels Jesus calls them hypocrites who have put aside the commandment of God for those of man. He is not looking for another building, another program, another ritual, another ceremony, another support group, or another ministry. He is looking for people whose lips have been touched, whose sin has been forgiven and taken away, who will say, "Send me, I'll go!"

He will support the heart that is completely His. So when we make our own plans, when we do it our way, we shouldn't expect victory, strength, or blessings. But when we do it His way, every day, expect Him to do exceeding abundantly above all that you could ask or think (Eph 3:20). Expect His unlimited favor, blessing, and power. Expect to be victorious and to excel in your faith, because He is God, and His power is unlimited. God sent Jesus to set you free!

Think about what you have studied today and whether you intend to live free consistently. Talk to your Father about what is on your mind.

Chapter Ten

THE DEVIL MADE ME…

People say, "The devil made me do it." But did he really? Can the influence of Satan keep you in bondage? Are you destined to be in captivity as long as you are on this earth? Can you be free of his tactics? Will binding and rebuking help? Or do you have to wait until Jesus comes back to be free?

Let's begin in the book of Job to see Satan's influences and some responses to him.

Job was the greatest of all the men in the east. He was a God-fearing man who was blameless and upright, turning away from evil. He had ten children, owned a lot of possessions, and had numerous servants. One day God had a visitor. Mark *God (Lord), Job* and *Satan*.

Now there was a day when the sons of God came to present themselves before the Lord, and Satan also came among them. The Lord said to Satan, "From where do you come?" Then Satan answered the Lord and said, "From roaming about on the earth and walking around on it." The Lord said to Satan, "Have you considered My servant Job? For there is no one like him on the earth, a blameless and upright man, fearing God and turning away from evil." Then Satan answered the Lord, "Does Job fear God for nothing? "Have You not made a hedge about him and his house and all that he has, on every side? You have blessed the work of his hands, and his possessions have increased in the land. "But put forth Your hand now and touch all that he has; he will surely curse You to Your face." Then the Lord said to Satan, "Behold, all that he has is in your power, only do not put forth your hand on him." So Satan departed from the presence of the Lord.

—Job 1:6–12

God had two questions for Satan. List them.

What did Satan know about Job and his relationship to God?

What did he think would make Job curse God?

What power did God give Satan over Job? What parameters? Is Satan in charge of bad and God in charge of good?

The attack began. Job's servants were killed. His livestock were attacked; some were taken, and some were consumed by fire from heaven. A great wind struck the four corners of the house, and his sons and daughters were killed when the house fell on them.

Then Job arose and tore his robe and shaved his head, and he fell to the ground and worshiped. He said, "Naked I came from my mother's womb, and naked I shall return there. The Lord gave and the Lord has taken away. Blessed be the name of the Lord." Through all this Job did not sin nor did he blame God.

—Job 1:20–22

The Devil Made Me...

Record Job's response.

Again there was a day when the sons of God came to present themselves before the Lord, and Satan also came among them to present himself before the Lord. The Lord said to Satan, "Where have you come from?" Then Satan answered the Lord and said, "From roaming about on the earth and walking around on it." The Lord said to Satan, "Have you considered My servant Job? For there is no one like him on the earth, a blameless and upright man fearing God and turning away from evil. And he still holds fast his integrity, although you incited Me against him to ruin him without cause." Satan answered the Lord and said, "Skin for skin! Yes, all that a man has he will give for his life. "However, put forth Your hand now, and touch his bone and his flesh; he will curse You to Your face." So the Lord said to Satan, "Behold, he is in your power, only spare his life." Then Satan went out from the presence of the Lord and smote Job with sore boils from the sole of his foot to the crown of his head. And he took a potsherd to scrape himself while he was sitting among the ashes. Then his wife said to him, "Do you still hold fast your integrity? Curse God and die!" But he said to her, "You speak as one of the foolish women speaks. Shall we indeed accept good from God and not accept adversity?" In all this Job did not sin with his lips.

—Job 2:1–10

Again Satan visits and God asks the same two questions. What does God say about Job and Himself?

How does Satan respond?

What does God do? Are there any limits?

What question does Mrs. Job ask, and what does she suggest to her husband?

What is Job's response? What two things does he say come from God?

Did you notice that he does not give Satan credit for doing anything?

Read and record under each Scripture listed below what you learn about Satan. Also write down the freedom you can have based on the truth of each verse.

Be angry, and yet do not sin; do not let the sun go down on your anger, and do not give the devil an opportunity.

—Ephesians 4:26–27

About Satan:

The Devil Made Me…

Your freedom:

The Lord's bond-servant must not be quarrelsome, but be kind to all, able to teach, patient when wronged, with gentleness correcting those who are in opposition, if perhaps God may grant them repentance leading to the knowledge of the truth, and they may come to their senses and escape from the snare of the devil, having been held captive by him to do his will.
—2 Timothy 2:24–26

About Satan:

Your freedom:

Record here how you can help someone escape his captivity. What must he know?

Therefore, since the children share in flesh and blood, He Himself likewise also partook of the same, that through death He might render powerless him who had the power of death, that is, the devil, and might free those who through fear of death were subject to slavery all their lives.
—Hebrews 2:14–15

Who was destroyed in this passage? What power did he have? When did it happen?

About Satan:

Your freedom:

Submit therefore to God. Resist the devil and he will flee from you.

—James 4:7

About Satan:

Your freedom:

What are you supposed to do before you resist the devil?

Be of sober spirit, be on the alert. Your adversary, the devil, prowls around like a roaring lion, seeking someone to devour. But resist him, firm in your faith, knowing that the same experiences of suffering are being accomplished by your brethren who are in the world.

—1 Peter 5:8–9

The Devil Made Me...

About Satan:

Your freedom:

The one who practices sin is of the devil; for the devil has sinned from the beginning. The Son of God appeared for this purpose, to destroy the works of the devil.
—1 John 3:8

About Satan:

Your freedom:

What did Jesus destroy? When?

You are from God, little children, and have overcome them; because greater is He who is in you than he who is in the world.
—1 John 4:4

About Satan:

Your freedom:

We know that no one who is born of God sins; but He who was born of God keeps him, and the evil one does not touch him. We know that we are of God, and that the whole world lies in the power of the evil one. And we know that the Son of God has come, and has given us understanding so that we may know Him who is true; and we are in Him who is true, in His Son Jesus Christ. This is the true God and eternal life.

—1 John 5:18–20

About Satan:

Your freedom:

Who is it that the wicked one cannot touch? Who lies under his power?

The Devil Made Me…

What have you learned today about the influence of the devil? Can he make you do anything? Can you be free from his tactics? Who is in charge? The wicked one does not have the right to touch you when you belong to Jesus. Aren't you glad Jesus came to set you free? Spend time thanking God for the freedom He provides. Write out your thoughts.

Who's to Blame?

Chapter Eleven

WHOM WILL GOD HOLD ACCOUNTABLE?

What if someone has been taught erroneously, whether out of ignorance, exploitation, or greed? What if the person has followed the erroneous teaching? Who is in bondage? Whom will God hold accountable, prophet or listener? Let's examine the Scriptures. Mark *Lord, people* and *prophets*.

> But, "Ah, Lord God!" I said, "Look, the prophets are telling them, 'You will not see the sword nor will you have famine, but I will give you lasting peace in this place.'" Then the Lord said to me, "The prophets are prophesying falsehood in My name. I have neither sent them nor commanded them nor spoken to them; they are prophesying to you a false vision, divination, futility and the deception of their own minds. Therefore thus says the Lord concerning the prophets who are prophesying in My name, although it was not I who sent them—yet they keep saying, 'There will be no sword or famine in this land'—by sword and famine those prophets shall meet their end! The people also to whom they are prophesying will be thrown out into the streets of Jerusalem because of the famine and the sword; and there will be no one to bury them—neither them, nor their wives, nor their sons, nor their daughters—for I will pour out their own wickedness on them."
>
> —Jeremiah 14:13–16

God told Jeremiah that He was going to call to account the sins of the people. They had repeatedly refused to listen to God (Jeremiah 13:10), had decided to walk in the stubbornness of their own hearts, and had gone after other gods.

God told Jeremiah that the people had forgotten Him and had trusted in falsehood, and as a result He was going to strip their skirts off and make them ashamed (verses 25–26). This is not the first time God used nakedness to shame the people. (See Genesis 3.) In fact, in Hebrews 4:13 all things are open and naked before Him.

God told Jeremiah not to pray for the welfare of the people. He was not going to accept their offering but was going to bring sword, famine, and pestilence.

What is Jeremiah's concern?

Who is to blame: the prophets, the people, or Jeremiah? Is there any bondage here?

Read Jeremiah 14:13–16 again and record God's response to Jeremiah and His judgment upon the prophets.

What is to happen to the people who have listened to and followed the false prophets? Could they have known truth? (See Jeremiah 13:10.)

Whom Will God Hold Accountable?

As you read, continue to mark *prophets, people* and *Lord* (and its pronouns)

"I have heard what the prophets have said who prophesy falsely in My name, saying, 'I had a dream, I had a dream!' How long? Is there anything in the hearts of the prophets who prophesy falsehood, even these prophets of the deception of their own heart, who intend to make My people forget My name by their dreams which they relate to one another, just as their fathers forgot My name because of Baal? The prophet who has a dream may relate his dream, but let him who has My word speak My word in truth. What does straw have in common with grain?" declares the Lord. "Is not My word like fire?" declares the Lord, "and like a hammer which shatters a rock? Therefore behold, I am against the prophets," declares the Lord, "who steal My words from each other. Behold, I am against the prophets," declares the Lord, "who use their tongues and declare, 'The Lord declares.' Behold, I am against those who have prophesied false dreams," declares the Lord, "and related them and led My people astray by their falsehoods and reckless boasting; yet I did not send them or command them, nor do they furnish this people the slightest benefit," declares the Lord.

—Jeremiah 23:25–32

Record what God says about His Word. What does He say about the prophets?

Don't miss the comparison of the Word of God and the prophet's dream.
Grain provides nourishment; straw does not. Grain sustains; straw does not.

"Now when this people or the prophet or a priest asks you saying, 'What is the oracle of the Lord?' then you shall say to them, 'What oracle?' The Lord declares, 'I will abandon you.' Then as for the prophet or the priest or the people who say, 'The oracle of the Lord,' I will bring punishment upon that man and his household. Thus will each of you say to his neighbor and to his brother, 'What has the Lord answered?' or, 'What has the Lord spoken?' For you will no longer remember the oracle of the Lord, because every man's own word will become the oracle, and you have perverted the words of the living God, the Lord of hosts, our God. Thus you will say to that prophet, 'What has the Lord answered you?' and, 'What has the Lord spoken?' For if you say, 'The oracle of the Lord!' surely thus says the Lord, 'Because you said this word, "The oracle of the Lord!" I have also sent to you, saying, "You shall not say, 'The oracle of the Lord!'"' Therefore behold, I will surely forget you and cast you away from My presence, along with the city which I gave you and your fathers."

—Jeremiah 23:33–39

What will happen to the prophet, the priest, and the people? Why will God bring this punishment on them? What have they done to His Word?

What does James 3:1 tell us about how God will judge His people?

> Let not many of you become teachers, my brethren, knowing that as such we will incur a stricter judgment.
>
> —James 3:1

> Remind them of these things, and solemnly charge them in the presence of God not to wrangle about words, which is useless and leads to the ruin of the hearers. Be diligent to present yourself approved to God as a workman who does not need to be ashamed, accurately handling the word of truth. But avoid worldly and empty chatter, for it will lead to further ungodliness, and their talk will spread like gangrene. Among them are Hymenaeus and Philetus, men who have gone astray from the truth saying that the resurrection has already taken place, and they upset the faith of some. Nevertheless, the firm foundation of God stands, having this seal, "The Lord knows those who are His," and, "Everyone who names the name of the Lord is to abstain from wickedness."
>
> —2 Timothy 2:14–19

Who is admonished to study the Word? What leads to ungodliness and the ruin of the hearers?

Two men are doing a lot of talking. How was their chatter described? From what had they gone astray, and what was the result?

Whom Will God Hold Accountable?

The firm foundation of God has been sealed. What two things are apparent?

All Scripture is inspired by God and profitable for teaching, for reproof, for correction, for training in righteousness; so that the man of God may be adequate, equipped for every good work.

—2 Tim 3:16–17

What four things will Scripture do? What will be the result for those who comply with all four points? Who will experience the result: priest, prophet, man, woman, boy, or girl?

Whom will God hold accountable: the one who taught the Word erroneously, whether intentionally or unintentionally, the one who heard it and followed it, or both? Was anyone in bondage here? Was anyone taken away captive? How could this captivity have been avoided? Hosea 4:6 (KJV) says, "My people are destroyed for lack of knowledge." What you don't know *can* hurt you; in fact, what you do not know can destroy you.

WORD STUDY

The meaning of the Hebrew word for "destroy," *damah,* **means "to cause to cease, to cut off, to be silent, perish; lay waste, a violent end."**

Don't self-destruct waiting for someone to feed you!

Lack of knowledge will kill you, and erroneous knowledge is the same as no knowledge at all. Only knowledge of the Word of God, in combination with faith, will free you from needless pain, keep you from being cut off from real truth, release you from fear, heal you, comfort you, strengthen you, and protect you. The Word will teach you who God is and how to walk in all His ways. Do you know His Word?

God wants His people free: ***"Let My people go."*** Are you in bondage because you do not know the truth? Are you headed for captivity, destruction, or a violent end? You can avoid it. Turn to the Word of God. You will know the truth and the truth will make you free (John 8:32).

Write out a plan to spend time daily in the Word.

Chapter Twelve

THE LAST SERMON

The last public sermon Jesus preached was not about His return for the church, or about living holy lives, or about how to witness so others could be saved. It was not about how to pray or fast, or how to disciple new believers. It was about false teachers and those they were manipulating.

There were two groups that provided guidance and authority for the people during Jesus' day. The scribes wrote the law and explained it in the schools and synagogues. The Pharisees, the dominant religious group, were separatists. Look in as Jesus speaks to the crowd and the disciples. Mark *scribes, Pharisees, they* and *servant*.

Then Jesus spoke to the crowds and to His disciples, saying: "The scribes and the Pharisees have seated themselves in the chair of Moses; therefore all that they tell you, do and observe, but do not do according to their deeds; for they say things and do not do them. They tie up heavy burdens and lay them on men's shoulders, but they themselves are unwilling to move them with so much as a finger. But they do all their deeds to be noticed by men; for they broaden their phylacteries and lengthen the tassels of their garments. They love the place of honor at banquets and the chief seats in the synagogues, and respectful greetings in the market places, and being called Rabbi by men. But do not be called Rabbi; for One is your Teacher, and you are all brothers. Do not call anyone on earth your father; for One is your Father, He who is in heaven. Do not be called leaders; for One is your Leader, that is, Christ. But the greatest among you shall be your servant. Whoever exalts himself shall be humbled; and whoever humbles himself shall be exalted.

—Matthew 23:1–12

List below how Jesus describe the scribes and Pharisees in the above passage. Who does Jesus say is the greatest and who will be exalted? Will the scribes and Pharisees be exalted? Why or why not?

"But woe to you, scribes and Pharisees, hypocrites, because you shut off the kingdom of heaven from people; for you do not enter in yourselves, nor do you allow those who are entering to go in. Woe to you, scribes and Pharisees, hypocrites, because you devour widows' houses, and for a pretense you make long prayers; therefore you will receive greater condemnation. Woe to you, scribes and Pharisees, hypocrites, because you travel around on sea and land to make one proselyte; and when he becomes one, you make him twice as much a son of hell as yourselves. Woe to you, blind guides, who say, 'Whoever swears by the temple, that is nothing; but whoever swears by the gold of the temple is obligated.' You fools and blind men! Which is more important, the gold or the temple that sanctified the gold? And, 'Whoever swears by the altar, that is nothing, but whoever swears by the offering on it, he is obligated.' You blind men, which is more important, the offering, or the altar that sanctifies the offering? Therefore, whoever swears by the altar, swears both by the altar and by everything on it. And whoever swears by the temple, swears both by the temple and by Him who dwells within it. And whoever swears by heaven, swears both by the throne of God and by Him who sits upon it.

—Matthew 23:13–22

WORD STUDY

The Greek word for "woe" is *ouai*, meaning "interjection of grief or indignation; of denouncing misery and pitying it; woe, alas!"

The Greek word for "hypocrite" is *hupokrites*, meaning "one who acts pretentiously, a counterfeit, a man who assumes and speaks or acts under a feigned character; a dissembler."

The Last Sermon

In the above passage Jesus says, "Woe to you" four times. In each of the four instances, who is involved in their hypocrisy? Who is being deceived? Are they believers? Include a Scripture reference with your answer.

As you read mark *scribes, Pharisees, hypocrites* and *you* the same way

"Woe to you, scribes and Pharisees, hypocrites! For you tithe mint and dill and cummin, and have neglected the weightier provisions of the law: justice and mercy and faithfulness; but these are the things you should have done without neglecting the others. You blind guides, who strain out a gnat and swallow a camel! Woe to you, scribes and Pharisees, hypocrites! For you clean the outside of the cup and of the dish, but inside they are full of robbery and self-indulgence. You blind Pharisee, first clean the inside of the cup and of the dish, so that the outside of it may become clean also. Woe to you, scribes and Pharisees, hypocrites! For you are like whitewashed tombs which on the outside appear beautiful, but inside they are full of dead men's bones and all uncleanness. So you, too, outwardly appear righteous to men, but inwardly you are full of hypocrisy and lawlessness. Woe to you, scribes and Pharisees, hypocrites! For you build the tombs of the prophets and adorn the monuments of the righteous, and say, 'If we had been living in the days of our fathers, we would not have been partners with them in shedding the blood of the prophets.' So you testify against yourselves, that you are sons of those who murdered the prophets. Fill up, then, the measure of the guilt of your fathers. You serpents, you brood of vipers, how will you escape the sentence of hell?"

—Matthew 23:23–33

There are four more woes. Continue your descriptive list of the scribes and Pharisees.

Thinking about all you have studied, go back to verse 13 and consider the definition of the word *shut*.

WORD STUDY

The Greek word for "shut" is *kleio*, meaning "to shut, to close." It is used metaphorically here to describe willfully preventing men from entering.

No wonder Jesus uses such strong language as "hypocrites," "fools," "blind guides," "son of hell," "self-indulgent robbers," "whitewashed tombs," "lawless," "sons of murderers," "serpents," and "brood of vipers." These people would not enter the kingdom and they were preventing others from entering.

Read what Luke adds in the parallel passage in Luke 11:52. Note what he says the scribes and Pharisees took away.

> Woe to you lawyers! For you have taken away the key of knowledge; you yourselves did not enter, and you hindered those who were entering.
>
> —Luke 11:52

Who is held accountable in these passages: the one who taught, those who listened, or both?

Think about all those who were "shut off" in Jesus' day and add all those who've been "shut off" since that time as a result of men and women misusing or not using Scripture. What will it take to move us to action? When will we stop the hypocrisy, the killings, the useless deaths? When our churches substitute the Word of God with music, feeding programs, classes on success, getting along with others, financial management, and career planning, the attendees do not get to know Jesus as their Savior, and they will die in their sins.

Matthew 23:15 says there were proselytes (converts to Judaism), but remember in verse 13 he says they were "shut off" from the kingdom. Our churches may be bulging at the seams, the Bible studies packed, the people friendly, and the services "anointed," but if the people do not know Jesus, they will die in their sins.

It is clear that this kind of religion is not in active pursuit of God, but rather the result of a major departure from God and His Word. When will we turn back to the true teaching of the Word of God and not the watered-down gospel of today? Where will the pursuit of the show, the spectacular, and the next "new thing" end? Where is the call for holiness and godly living? When will we teach and live the simple truth of the Word of God, with nothing added and nothing taken away? When will we stand up and be the exemplary people made righteous by the blood of Jesus that we should be?

> Therefore, behold, I am sending you prophets and wise men and scribes; some of them you will kill and crucify, and some of them you will scourge in your synagogues, and persecute from city to city, so that upon you may fall the guilt of all the righteous blood shed on earth,

The Last Sermon

from the blood of righteous Abel to the blood of Zechariah, the son of Berechiah, whom you murdered between the temple and the altar. Truly I say to you, all these things will come upon this generation. Jerusalem, Jerusalem, who kills the prophets and stones those who are sent to her! How often I wanted to gather your children together, the way a hen gathers her chicks under her wings, and you were unwilling. Behold, your house is being left to you desolate! For I say to you, from now on you will not see Me until you say, 'Blessed is he who comes in the name of the Lord!'"

—Matthew 23:34–39

What is Jesus' prophecy in these verses? What does He want to do with the children? What is the people's response?

God offered the kingdom. He gave His Son. He loved the world. He longs for all to come, to believe, to follow Jesus, the Christ. But most are not willing. What about you? Are you truly His or are you still in bondage to sin? If you are in bondage, He can set you free. Are you willing to be set free? Jesus said to Israel, "Blessed is He who comes in the name of the Lord." Will you invite Him in?

If you are already His, are you living free or are you held hostage by something, someone, or yourself because you do not know the truth or will not acknowledge or obey it? Get into God's Word. Read it, study it, meditate on it, live it, and tell it!

O Lord, surely I am Your servant, I am Your servant, the son of Your handmaid, You have loosed my bonds. To You I shall offer a sacrifice of thanksgiving, And call upon the name of the Lord.

—Psalm 116:16–17

Whatever your situation may be, right now is a great time to call upon the name of the Lord.

Recognizing The Bondages

Chapter Thirteen

SELF-INFLICTED: RECOGNIZE IT!

Many people cannot see that they are in bondage. They do not realize that they have been taken captive by anything. Many deny there is a problem. They would never admit they are wrong, and they hate being told what to do.

Some have made a lie their refuge and deception their hiding place (Isaiah 28:15). In order for freedom to be experienced, the bondage, their sin, must be recognized, acknowledged, and dealt with. As we look at the sin and bondage that engulfed David, we will see the freedom he experiences when he acknowledges and deals with his sin.

David was ruddy, with beautiful eyes and a handsome appearance, when the Lord sent Samuel to anoint Israel's second king. David's father, Jesse, made seven of his sons pass before Samuel, but the Lord had not chosen any of them. Finally David, the youngest son, was called in from tending sheep and the Lord said, "Arise, anoint him, for this is he" (1 Samuel 16:12). Israel's first king, Saul, was still reigning at the time.

David learned many lessons from that point on. He wrestled with lions and bears and fought men like Goliath. He became good friends with Jonathan, Saul's son, and married Saul's daughter, Michal. He became a mighty warrior, slaying thousands.

Saul was not happy with the recognition David was getting from the people and became his archenemy, even seeking to kill him. While David was on the run from Saul, he had opportunities to kill him, but he didn't.

Eventually Saul and Jonathan were killed. David mourned their deaths, chanting a lament over them (2 Samuel 1). Then he ordered the one who had killed them to be slain. David, this mighty man of God, whom God calls a man after His own heart, experienced some serious problems.

In 2 Samuel 11, the time is the spring of the year, when kings go out to battle. David, however, stayed in Jerusalem. One evening, from the roof of his house, he saw a woman bathing. Although he was told she was married, he sent for her. He lay with her, she conceived, and she sent him a message saying, "I am pregnant." David sent for her husband, Uriah, who was in the battle, to come home and be with his wife. But Uriah was a loyal warrior and would not spend time with his wife while the other men were in the heat of the battle. So David sent Uriah back to the battle with a note for Joab, the commander of David's army. David instructed Joab to put Uriah in the front lines, where he would surely be killed. Uriah's death in battle was followed by a time of mourning, after which David sent for Bathsheba and she became his wife. But the thing that David had done was evil in the sight of the Lord.

> Then the Lord sent Nathan to David. And he came to him and said, "There were two men in one city, the one rich and the other poor. The rich man had a great many flocks and herds. But the poor man had nothing except one little ewe lamb Which he bought and nourished; And it grew up together with him and his children. It would eat of his bread and drink of his cup and lie in his bosom, And was like a daughter to him. Now a traveler came to the rich man, And he was unwilling to take from his own flock or his own herd, To prepare for the wayfarer who had come to him; Rather he took the poor man's ewe lamb and prepared it for the man who had come to him." Then David's anger burned greatly against the man, and he said to Nathan, "As the Lord lives, surely the man who has done this deserves to die. He must make restitution for the lamb fourfold, because he did this thing and had no compassion."
>
> —2 Samuel 12:1–6

Why does Nathan go to David?

Summarize below the story of the rich man and the poor man.

Self-inflicted: Recognize It! 93

What is David's response? What judgment does he make and why?

Nathan has painted the picture and David has passed judgment.

Nathan then said to David, "You are the man! Thus says the Lord God of Israel, 'It is I who anointed you king over Israel and it is I who delivered you from the hand of Saul. I also gave you your master's house and your master's wives into your care, and I gave you the house of Israel and Judah; and if that had been too little, I would have added to you many more things like these! Why have you despised the word of the Lord by doing evil in His sight? You have struck down Uriah the Hittite with the sword, have taken his wife to be your wife, and have killed him with the sword of the sons of Ammon. Now therefore, the sword shall never depart from your house, because you have despised Me and have taken the wife of Uriah the Hittite to be your wife.' Thus says the Lord, 'Behold, I will raise up evil against you from your own household; I will even take your wives before your eyes and give them to your companion, and he will lie with your wives in broad daylight. Indeed you did it secretly, but I will do this thing before all Israel, and under the sun.'" Then David said to Nathan, "I have sinned against the Lord." And Nathan said to David, "The Lord also has taken away your sin; you shall not die. However, because by this deed you have given occasion to the enemies of the Lord to blaspheme, the child also that is born to you shall surely die."

—2 Samuel 12:7–14

The basis of Nathan's confrontation is "God said…" Record what God says He has done for David.

What did David despise? What specific sins are listed?

What is God's judgment for David? List the specific consequences.

What does David finally admit?

God took the child that Bathsheba conceived. David comforts her and she has another son, Solomon. What we do not see in this 2 Samuel passage is David's brokenness. But after Nathan came to David, he poured out his heart before the Lord. (See Psalm 51.)

Be gracious to me, O God, according to Your lovingkindness; According to the greatness of Your compassion blot out my transgressions. Wash me thoroughly from my iniquity And cleanse me from my sin. For I know my transgressions, And my sin is ever before me. Against You, You only, I have sinned And done what is evil in Your sight, So that You are justified when You speak And blameless when You judge. Behold, I was brought forth in iniquity, And in sin my mother conceived me. Behold, You desire truth in the innermost being, And in the hidden part You will make me know wisdom. Purify me with hyssop, and I shall be clean; Wash me, and I shall be whiter than snow. Make me to hear joy and gladness, Let the bones which You have broken rejoice. Hide Your face from my sins And blot out all my iniquities.
—Psalm 51:1–9

David uses three different Hebrew words to describe his actions.

WORD STUDY

The Hebrew word for "transgression" is *pesha,* meaning "rebellion, sin, transgression, trespass." The idea here is a willful deviation from righteousness.

The Hebrew word for "iniquity" is *avon,* meaning "perversity; i.e., (moral) evil:–fault, iniquity, mischief, punishment (of iniquity), sin."

The Hebrew word for "sin" is *chattaah,* meaning "punishment (of sin), purifying (-fication for sin), sin (-ner, offering)." The idea here is to miss the mark.

Self-inflicted: Recognize It!

From these definitions, It is clear that David not only admits his sin and rebellion, he also admits he missed the mark and that the sin was perverse and willful. He acknowledges the punishment, the consequences, and the purification needed for his sins. From the passage above, record his confession and his requests to God.

David knows enough about his sin and about God to use covenant terms like *lovingkindness* and *mercy*. He is asking God to be merciful, to have pity upon him, to be gracious and to give him favor.

WORD STUDY

The Hebrew word for "blot out" is *machah*, meaning "to abolish, blot out, destroy, full of marrow, put out, reach unto, utterly, wipe (away, out)."

David asks for mercy. He also wants God to totally get rid of his sin. Can you feel his heart? He is looking for complete release from the bondage.

> Create in me a clean heart, O God, And renew a steadfast spirit within me. Do not cast me away from Your presence And do not take Your Holy Spirit from me. Restore to me the joy of Your salvation And sustain me with a willing spirit. Then I will teach transgressors Your ways, And sinners will be converted to You. Deliver me from bloodguiltiness, O God, the God of my salvation; Then my tongue will joyfully sing of Your righteousness. O Lord, open my lips, That my mouth may declare Your praise. For You do not delight in sacrifice, otherwise I would give it; You are not pleased with burnt offering. The sacrifices of God are a broken spirit; A broken and a contrite heart, O God, You will not despise. By Your favor do good to Zion; Build the walls of Jerusalem. Then You will delight in righteous sacrifices, In burnt offering and whole burnt offering; Then young bulls will be offered on Your altar.
>
> —Psalm 51:10–19

Look at David's request. Can you see the breach in his relationship with God because of the bondage of sin? List the areas that David mentions.

David asks God to restore the joy of his salvation. After restoration, what will David do?

A Psalm of David. A Maskil. How blessed is he whose transgression is forgiven, Whose sin is covered! 2 How blessed is the man to whom the Lord does not impute iniquity, And in whose spirit there is no deceit!

—Psalm 32:1

David uses the same three words for sin in these verses. How does he describe himself and why?

Read the last two verses of this Psalm.

Many are the sorrows of the wicked, But he who trusts in the Lord, lovingkindness shall surround him. Be glad in the Lord and rejoice, you righteous ones; And shout for joy, all you who are upright in heart.

—Psalm 32:10–11

Record what you see about the wicked. Also record what you see about those who trust in the Lord, those who are righteous, and those who are upright in heart.

Self-inflicted: Recognize It!

The Lord:

The Righteous:

The Wicked:

Has God painted a picture for you today? Could you use His mercy and lovingkindness in your situation? He is ready to blot out your sin, transgression, or iniquity and give you a clean heart and restore to you the joy of your salvation. Are you willing to come to Him with a broken spirit and a contrite heart? Is your soul in prison today? Ask Him for His perfect release.

> Bring my soul out of prison, so that I may give thanks to Your name; the righteous will surround me, For You will deal bountifully with me.
>
> —Psalm 142:7

Ask Him!

Chapter Fourteen
_____

FROM OTHERS: CHECK IT!

By the time Peter wrote his second letter to believers of like faith (2 Peter 1:1), he was nearing the end of his life. Following the instruction Jesus had given him to "feed my sheep" (John 21:15), Peter wrote to remind them of things they already knew, of truth that had already been established (1:12). He wanted them to remember the words spoken by the prophets and the disciples (2 Peter 3:2). He wanted them to remember these things even after he was gone. False teachers had arisen and he did not want these Christians to fall from their steadfastness, so he encouraged them to make sure of their calling and to grow in the grace and knowledge of Jesus Christ.

> But false prophets also arose among the people, just as there will also be false teachers among you, who will secretly introduce destructive heresies, even denying the Master who bought them, bringing swift destruction upon themselves. Many will follow their sensuality, and because of them the way of the truth will be maligned; and in their greed they will exploit you with false words; their judgment from long ago is not idle, and their destruction is not asleep.
> —2 Peter 2:1–3

Where will the false prophets and teachers come from? Who will follow them?

List what they will do:

To themselves　　　　　　　　　**Why?**
_____　　　　_____
_____　　　　_____
_____　　　　_____

To others　　　　　　　　　　　**How?**
_____　　　　_____
_____　　　　_____
_____　　　　_____

If these false teachers deny the Master, malign truth, are greedy, and exploit people, they are bringing destruction upon themselves. So why would the people follow?

> …and especially those who indulge the flesh in its corrupt desires and despise authority. Daring, self-willed, they do not tremble when they revile angelic majesties, whereas angels who are greater in might and power do not bring a reviling judgment against them before the Lord. But these, like unreasoning animals, born as creatures of instinct to be captured and killed, reviling where they have no knowledge, will in the destruction of those creatures also be destroyed, suffering wrong as the wages of doing wrong. They count it a pleasure to revel in the daytime. They are stains and blemishes, reveling in their deceptions, as they carouse with you, having eyes full of adultery that never cease from sin, enticing unstable souls, having a heart trained in greed, accursed children; forsaking the right way, they have gone astray, having followed the way of Balaam, the son of Beor, who loved the wages of unrighteousness; but he received a rebuke for his own transgression, for a mute donkey, speaking with a voice of a man, restrained the madness of the prophet.
>
> —2 Peter 2:10–16

From Others: Check It!

Describe these false teachers.

Read the passage again. What will happen to the false teachers/prophets? What do they really know? What kind of people are being enticed by them?

WORD STUDY

The Greek word for "entice" is *deleazo*, meaning "to bait or trap."

Why would anyone follow these false prophets? How can they captivate so many?

These are springs without water and mists driven by a storm, for whom the black darkness has been reserved. For speaking out arrogant words of vanity they entice by fleshly desires, by sensuality, those who barely escape from the ones who live in error, promising them freedom while they themselves are slaves of corruption; for by what a man is overcome, by this he is enslaved.

—2 Peter 2:17–19

Record more description of the false teachers and prophets.

How do they entice (or trap) people? Is it by what they say or what they do or both?

What kind of promises do they make? Notice that they themselves are in bondage.

According to what you have read so far, can a believer be enticed? How could you avoid being entrapped? How would you identify the false? What did Peter want believers to remember even after he was gone?

Peter's final words of this short letter were a reminder that Christ was going to fulfill His promise and return. In the meantime believers were to conduct themselves in holy conduct and godliness, looking forward to that day in great anticipation.

> Therefore, beloved, since you look for these things, be diligent to be found by Him in peace, spotless and blameless, and regard the patience of our Lord as salvation; just as also our beloved brother Paul, according to the wisdom given him, wrote to you, as also in all his letters, speaking in them of these things, in which are some things hard to understand, which the untaught and unstable distort, as they do also the rest of the Scriptures, to their own destruction. You therefore, beloved, knowing this beforehand, be on your guard so that you are not carried away by the error of unprincipled men and fall from your own steadfastness, but grow in the grace and knowledge of our Lord and Savior Jesus Christ. To Him be the glory, both now and to the day of eternity. Amen.
>
> —2 Peter 3:14–18

What does Peter say about the false teachers and prophets?

From Others: Check It!

List what Peter tells the believers to do. According to the passage, how could they avoid being carried away and falling? What is paramount to their growth and being able to stand (not fall)?

Jude gives a similar description of those leading believers astray and into bondage. He also provides instruction for the saints.

> Beloved, while I was making every effort to write you about our common salvation, I felt the necessity to write to you appealing that you contend earnestly for the faith which was once for all handed down to the saints. For certain persons have crept in unnoticed, those who were long beforehand marked out for this condemnation, ungodly persons who turn the grace of our God into licentiousness and deny our only Master and Lord, Jesus Christ.
> —Jude 1:3–4

What is the instruction?

How did these "certain persons" get in? Were they believers? How do you know?

> These are grumblers, finding fault, following after their own lusts; they speak arrogantly, flattering people for the sake of gaining an advantage. But you, beloved, ought to remember the words that were spoken beforehand by the apostles of our Lord Jesus Christ, that they were saying to you, "In the last time there will be mockers, following after their own ungodly lusts." These are the ones who cause divisions, worldly-minded, devoid of the Spirit.
> —Jude 1:16–19

How are the deceivers described?

How do these deceivers captivate God's people? What does Jude tell the people to remember? What was the warning of the apostles?

> But you, beloved, building yourselves up on your most holy faith, praying in the Holy Spirit, keep yourselves in the love of God, waiting anxiously for the mercy of our Lord Jesus Christ to eternal life. And have mercy on some, who are doubting; save others, snatching them out of the fire; and on some have mercy with fear, hating even the garment polluted by the flesh.
> —Jude 1:20–23

List the instructions to the people.

> Now to Him who is able to keep you from stumbling, and to make you stand in the presence of His glory blameless with great joy, to the only God our Savior, through Jesus Christ our Lord, be glory, majesty, dominion and authority, before all time and now and forever. Amen.
> —Jude 1:24–25

Record Jude's final exhortation.

Are you willing, as Jude says, to build yourself up on your most holy faith? Since faith comes by hearing the Word, are you willing to spend time in the Word, growing in the grace and knowledge of our Lord and Savior, Jesus Christ? You can escape the corruption of the world if you stand on His magnificent and precious promises (2 Peter 1:3). You can avoid being captivated, misled, exploited, enticed, and carried away by the error of unprincipled men. Be on your guard, and grow!

Chapter Fifteen

UNDER THE CIRCUMSTANCES: WATCH IT!

Are you dealing with what appears to be an impossible situation? Are you facing circumstances that are too difficult to handle? Have you become weary and frustrated? Are you doing the best you can yet the situation never gets any better? Do you find yourself fighting discouragement and despair?

If this is the way you are feeling, be encouraged! Although you may feel overwhelmed, focus on the Word. God is not shaken or surprised. He is never taken off guard. He does not have to think about what to do. He has not lost control of your circumstances. He promises to work all things for the good of those who love Him. Your situation may seem impossible to you, but nothing is too hard for God.

The problem is, most of us like to control our circumstances. We like to be on top of those things that impact us, like our health, family, children, jobs, and financial issues. The reality is, much of what we deal with on a daily basis is out of our control.

No matter how impossible the situation may seem to you, focus on the Word. Christ is in this with you and He will provide a way of escape, not so you can get out, but that you may bear it (1 Corinthians 10:13). When God's solution to your problem is not to remove it, remember, His grace is sufficient for you, for power is perfected in weakness. He provides the power to bear up under your problem, and at the same time the ability to rise above it. He promises in Psalm 138:8 to perfect that which concerns you.

Listen to what He says in Matthew 6:26 "Look at the birds of the air, that they do not sow, nor reap nor gather into barns, and yet your heavenly Father feeds them. Are you not worth much more than they?" If God takes such good care of the birds, don't you think he can take care of you, His most precious creation?

God has not placed us in a sterile environment and commanded us to live in holiness. He has placed us in circumstances that require total dependence upon Him and commanded us to live holy. He has given you all that you require to accomplish everything He has assigned. If you are not doing well under your present circumstances, why not try doing things God's way?

John 5 describes a feast day in Jerusalem. In the city was a pool called Bethesda. In the five porticoes there lay many who were sick, blind, lame, and withered. They were waiting for the moving of the waters. An angel of the Lord would go down at certain seasons into the pool and stir up the water. The first one who stepped in after the stirring would be made well.

> A man was there who had been ill for thirty-eight years. When Jesus saw him lying there, and knew that he had already been a long time in that condition, He said to him, "Do you wish to get well?" The sick man answered Him, "Sir, I have no man to put me into the pool when the water is stirred up, but while I am coming, another steps down before me." Jesus said to him, "Get up, pick up your pallet and walk." Immediately the man became well, and picked up his pallet and began to walk. Now it was the Sabbath on that day.
>
> —John 5:5–9

How long had the man been sick?

What does Jesus ask him?

Can you think of anything a person would have to give up just to be free?

Under the Circumstances: Watch It!

What three things did Jesus tell the man to do?

Do you wonder why Jesus asked him that question? I do. The man's answer should be obvious, but what does he say?

Did the man avoid Jesus' question? Here he is, face to face with the Healer, and he does not really answer the question. Instead he offers an excuse. His defense lies in a thirty-eight-year-old solution that has never materialized.

Do you wish to get well? There is no pain too deep, no damage too extensive that the hand of God cannot reach it. But healing must be done God's way.

Our weaknesses are occasions for God to show Himself strong on our behalf. We must ask God to search us and our thoughts, and if He finds any hurtful way within us, to lead us in the everlasting way (Psalm 139:23–24).

But we are not to nurse or rehearse our hurts, the shortcomings, or failures. We are to forget those things that are behind, reach toward what lies ahead, and press toward the mark for the prize of the high call of God in Christ Jesus (Philippians 3:13–14). That does not happen by sitting at the pool waiting for someone to put you in the water, to work out your problem.

Do you wish to get out of bondage? If you find yourself face to face with bitterness, unforgiveness, anger, disappointment, and affliction, remember these feelings are not new or unique to you. Confess, repent, and move on. In 2 Timothy, Paul tells Timothy to retain the standard of sound words and to guard the treasure that has been entrusted to him. He tells him to handle the Word accurately and to continue in the things he has learned.

When the tough times come, we are to hold on to our faith…not head knowledge, not common sense, not what everyone else is doing, but what we have learned to be true from the Word of God.

Remember…

- God is faithful. Ask Him to make you aware of all the ways He proves His faithfulness to you daily.

- God has blessed you with all spiritual blessings in heavenly places, regardless of how things may look.
- God has given you all things that pertain to life and godliness, so put aside thoughts of low self-esteem.
- God has given you the ability to escape the corruption of the world when you stand on His promises.
- God has redeemed you from the guilt of sin, so get rid of false guilt.
- God has not given you a spirit of fear, so cast fear aside.
- God is a forgiving God, so go ahead and confess your sins.
- God is sovereign, so allow Him to work in you both to will and to do of His good pleasure.

Jesus said to the man, "Do you wish to be well? Then, arise take up your pallet and walk!" What about you? Are you ready to walk into the freedom that Christ has made available?

On another day Jesus was coming down from the mountain. A crowd met him there, and a man from the crowd asked Him to look at his son. The boy was possessed with a spirit and the disciples had tried casting it out but were not successful.

> And He asked his father, "How long has this been happening to him?" And he said, "From childhood. It has often thrown him both into the fire and into the water to destroy him. But if You can do anything, take pity on us and help us!" And Jesus said to him, "'If You can?' All things are possible to him who believes." Immediately the boy's father cried out and said, "I do believe; help my unbelief."
>
> —Mark 9:21–24

What was Jesus' question to the father?

What does the father want Jesus to do? Does he seem to be overwhelmingly confident that Jesus can help them? Write out his "if" statement.

Under the Circumstances: Watch It!

What is Jesus' response?

How does the father respond when Jesus presses him about his belief?

If you are going to consistently walk in freedom, you must believe that God can and that He will do what He says.

WORD STUDY

"Believe" here is *pisteuo,* from *pistis,* and means "to be firmly persuaded, have faith in; believe." The idea is to have complete dependence on God. This firm persuasion is life transforming.

"Unbelief" is *apistia,* from *apistos,* meaning "not trusting God, uncertain, not confident of His power, untrustworthy."

We have faith for salvation and we are freed from our sins, but God wants us to have faith for our everyday issues. We are to live by faith (Romans 1:17).

What does the following passage say about doubting?

> But if any of you lacks wisdom, let him ask of God, who gives to all generously and without reproach, and it will be given to him. But he must ask in faith without any doubting, for the one who doubts is like the surf of the sea, driven and tossed by the wind. For that man ought not to expect that he will receive anything from the Lord.
>
> —James 1:5–7

What will you receive from the Lord if you doubt? Why?

Kate, a woman in our Bible Study who is being tremendously used by God, has severe asthma and terminal lung disease, with only 30 percent lung capacity. Seven years ago, she was told she needed a lung transplant. Yet she lives a very alive and pretty independent life. A routine dental appointment one day resulted in a referral to an oral surgeon. She put it off for a year and a half out of what she describes as "the big fear." She was afraid that when the surgeon numbed her mouth to pull the tooth, she would panic and not be able to breathe. But God arranged a series of circumstances to force her to face this fear. She says…

"I heard Charles Stanley on TV Sunday morning before church, and his message was on fear. It was as if the Holy Spirit said my name because it was so real to me. He was saying if there is a fear in your life and you are avoiding it, God would allow circumstances in your life until you face it.

Thursday I went to Bible study, where we are studying Deuteronomy, *Precept upon Precept*. We are where the Israelites have to face the Anakims before going into the Promised Land. They had to wander in the desert forty years because they wouldn't face these giants to begin with. I started crying! I knew I had to face my fear. My husband was with me, my friend Patty was with me, and the dentist and nurse are Christians. What more could I ask? It was not until I said, "Father, You promised to never leave me or forsake me," that I was able to relax and let go. My blood pressure went back to normal, the top of my mouth did not get numb, my breathing was fine, and the tooth came out.

God showed me something that day, just like He always does. I am not able on my own to conquer these fears. Whether a giant or a little thing, only with God's help and His Spirit within me can I do such things as these. Not only did my tooth come out, but my husband (who is not saved) saw that God delivered me. I thank Him for saving me and setting me free from myself!"

Even daily circumstances can keep us in bondage if we do not believe our Lord. In both large and small things, God always has a plan for our lives and for those we come in contact with.

You can have victory and peace when circumstances and relationships in your life are out of control and trouble is troubling you.

Do you not know? Have you not heard? The Everlasting God, the Lord, the Creator of the ends of the earth Does not become weary or tired. His understanding is inscrutable. He gives strength to the weary, And to him who lacks might He increases power. Though youths grow weary and tired, And vigorous young men stumble badly, Yet those who wait for the Lord Will gain new strength; They will mount up with wings like eagles, They will run and not get tired, They will walk and not become weary.

—Isaiah 40:28–31

Under the Circumstances: Watch It!

I started a list of God's part and my part. Add to the list from the Isaiah 40 passage above.

FOCUS ON THE WORD...GOD'S PART

1. God is in charge. He never loses control.
2. Nothing is too hard for God.
3. He loves you with an everlasting love.
4.
5.
6.
7.

FOCUS ON THE WORD...YOUR PART

1. Turn it over to God—He wants you to depend on Him.
2. Follow His directions—respond in obedience.
3. Believe He is working for your good and His glory.
4. Wait on the Lord.
5.
6.
7.

Do you see the relationship between believing and freedom? God's Word will perform its work in you if you believe (1 Thessalonians 2:13). Will you believe this truth that God has shown you today? If you need to ask God to help your unbelief, do so! Remember, His demand is *"Let My people go,"* and He came in the flesh to set you free.

Chapter Sixteen

FREEDOM'S CLOAK: WEAR IT!

In John 8, Jesus is in the temple, addressing several issues. While He is teaching, the scribes and Pharisees, who constantly sought to discredit Him and His teachings, bring one accusation after another. First they accuse a woman caught in adultery, then they accuse Jesus of lying. Jesus calmly handles each issue and then continues to teach. He tells them that He is going away, that He is from above, and that if they do not believe that "I am He, you will die in your sins" (John 8:24). He told them that God had sent Him and that He (Jesus) did nothing of His own initiative, but spoke only what the Father taught Him. Most of His listeners did not understand that Jesus was talking about God the Father. But as He spoke, many came to believe. Read John 8:31–38 circle the word *free* and underline *truth*.

> So Jesus was saying to those Jews who had believed Him, "If you continue in My word, then you are truly disciples of Mine; and you will know the truth, and the truth will make you free." They answered Him, "We are Abraham's descendants and have never yet been enslaved to anyone; how is it that You say, 'You will become free'?" Jesus answered them, "Truly, truly, I say to you, everyone who commits sin is the slave of sin. The slave does not remain in the house forever; the son does remain forever. So if the Son makes you free, you will be free indeed. I know that you are Abraham's descendants; yet you seek to kill Me, because My word has no place in you. I speak the things which I have seen with My Father; therefore you also do the things which you heard from your father."
>
> —John 8:31–38

Make a list of what Jesus says about being free.

What connection does Jesus make between freedom, truth, and the Word?

What must people know to be free? How will they know truth?

What will make them free? Who will make them free?

Notice how the people respond to Jesus' statement on freedom. They do not acknowledge their bondage, though they had been enslaved (in Egypt, Babylon, and Assyria) and were now enslaved to sin. According to the passage above and the definition below, who is the true disciple?

WORD STUDY

The Greek word for "disciple" is *mathetes* and means more in the New Testament than a mere pupil or learner. It is an adherent who accepts the instruction given to him and makes it his rule of conduct.

According to the passage above, why are the people responding as they are? Do they know truth? Are they free? Are they continuing in the Word?

Freedom's Cloak: Wear It!

WORD STUDY

The Greek word for "free" in this verse is *eleuteróo*, meaning "to make free, liberate from the power and punishment of sin, the result of redemption."

Read the following and mark the words *God, truth,* and *word.*

They answered and said to Him, "Abraham is our father." Jesus said to them, "If you are Abraham's children, do the deeds of Abraham. But as it is, you are seeking to kill Me, a man who has told you the truth, which I heard from God; this Abraham did not do. You are doing the deeds of your father." They said to Him, "We were not born of fornication; we have one Father: God." Jesus said to them, "If God were your Father, you would love Me, for I proceeded forth and have come from God, for I have not even come on My own initiative, but He sent Me. Why do you not understand what I am saying? It is because you cannot hear My word."
—John 8:39–43

What does Jesus say about their deeds?

What does Jesus say about God? What does He say about their father?

Why does Jesus say they cannot understand?

Go back to verses John 8:31–38. Who are the true disciples and what will knowing truth do? Does this help you understand why so many are in bondage today?

Read on, marking *God* and *truth*.

"You are of your father the devil, and you want to do the desires of your father. He was a murderer from the beginning, and does not stand in the truth because there is no truth in him. Whenever he speaks a lie, he speaks from his own nature, for he is a liar and the father of lies. "But because I speak the truth, you do not believe Me. Which one of you convicts Me of sin? If I speak truth, why do you not believe Me? He who is of God hears the words of God; for this reason you do not hear them, because you are not of God."

—John 8:44–47

Who does Jesus say their father is? Why?

How is their father described? How does the description of their father show up in them, his children? Go back to verse 31 to get the full picture.

Remembering that truth frees, according to verses John 8:44–47, what is keeping them from freedom?

Freedom's Cloak: Wear It!

According to this passage above and the definition below, why can't they hear the words of God?

WORD STUDY

The Greek word for "hear" in this verse is *akouo*, meaning "to hear someone or something; to obey."

This group could be freed from the bondage of sin, from the power and punishment of sin, if they would just believe and walk in obedience to the truth. How true of many today who refuse to believe the truth of the Word and be made free, who refuse to accept Jesus who makes free. What will happen to those who do not believe? Read John 8:24 and write out your answer.

> Therefore I said to you that you will die in your sins; for unless you believe that I am He, you will die in your sins.
>
> —John 8:24

How does God want you to respond to what He has shown you today?

Jesus' Assignment: "Break the Yoke"

Chapter Seventeen
───────────────

SHEPHERDS AND SHEEP

Do you realize that believing or not believing in Jesus is a matter of life or death? Although not all of Jesus' activities were written in the book of John, what is there is "written so that you may believe that Jesus is the Christ, the Son of God; and that believing you may have life in His name" (John 20:31). We know from Luke 19:10 that Jesus was sent to seek and to save the lost. From Acts 4:12 we know that there is no other name under heaven by which men can be saved. From John 3:16 we know that God sent Jesus so that anyone who believes will not perish.

Did you also know that Jesus saved us so that the bondage and power of sin would be broken to allow us to live freely on a daily basis? Free from self-inflicted bondages, the bondages of the world, and bondages from other people. We can live free from the battle, whether physical, mental, emotional, intellectual, psychological, moral, or spiritual.

Most people don't seem to know this freedom exists. Do you? Will you share it with unbelievers so they will not perish? Will you share it with those who are saved so they can live freely?

The problem exists both with leaders and followers. Look at what God says about the shepherds of Israel and the sheep in Ezekiel's day.

> "Son of man, prophesy against the shepherds of Israel. Prophesy and say to those shepherds, 'Thus says the Lord GOD, "Woe, shepherds of Israel who have been feeding themselves! Should not the shepherds feed the flock? You eat the fat and clothe yourselves with the wool, you slaugh-

ter the fat sheep without feeding the flock. Those who are sickly you have not strengthened, the diseased you have not healed, the broken you have not bound up, the scattered you have not brought back, nor have you sought for the lost; but with force and with severity you have dominated them. They were scattered for lack of a shepherd, and they became food for every beast of the field and were scattered. My flock wandered through all the mountains and on every high hill; My flock was scattered over all the surface of the earth, and there was no one to search or seek for them."'"

—Ezekiel 34:2–6

What is the condition of the sheep? What are the shepherds doing or not doing?

Which sheep are receiving the most benefit: the fat sheep or the others?

Where are the sheep? Are any lost? Why? Is anyone looking for them?

Thus says the Lord GOD, "Behold, I am against the shepherds, and I will demand My sheep from them and make them cease from feeding sheep. So the shepherds will not feed themselves anymore, but I will deliver My flock from their mouth, so that they will not be food for them." For thus says the Lord GOD, "Behold, I Myself will search for My sheep and seek them out. As a shepherd cares for his herd in the day when he is among his scattered sheep, so I will care for My sheep and will deliver them from all the places to which they were scattered on a cloudy and gloomy day. I will feed My flock and I will lead them to rest," declares the Lord God. "I will seek the lost, bring back the scattered, bind up the broken and strengthen the sick; but the fat and the strong I will destroy. I will feed them with judgment."

—Ezekiel 34:10–16

Shepherds and Sheep

What is God's plan for the shepherds?

What does God Himself plan to do?

How are the sheep described?

"As for you, My flock, thus says the Lord GOD, 'Behold, I will judge between one sheep and another, between the rams and the male goats. Is it too slight a thing for you that you should feed in the good pasture, that you must tread down with your feet the rest of your pastures? Or that you should drink of the clear waters, that you must foul the rest with your feet? As for My flock, they must eat what you tread down with your feet and drink what you foul with your feet!'" Therefore, thus says the Lord GOD to them, "Behold, I, even I, will judge between the fat sheep and the lean sheep. Because you push with side and with shoulder, and thrust at all the weak with your horns until you have scattered them abroad, therefore, I will deliver My flock, and they will no longer be a prey; and I will judge between one sheep and another. Then I will set over them one shepherd, My servant David, and he will feed them; he will feed them himself and be their shepherd. And I, the Lord, will be their God, and My servant David will be prince among them; I the Lord have spoken."

—Ezekiel 34:17–24

The sheep were prey for the shepherds, but they had also become prey for one another. Record what the sheep were doing and what God planned to do about it.

God promised to set one shepherd over Israel, David, to make a covenant of peace with them and to cause showers of blessings to come upon them.

Read verse 27 and the last two verses in the chapter.

"Also the tree of the field will yield its fruit and the earth will yield its increase, and they will be secure on their land. Then they will know that I am the Lord, when I have broken the bars of their yoke and have delivered them from the hand of those who enslaved them. Then they will know that I, the Lord their God, am with them, and that they, the house of Israel, are My people," declares the Lord God. "As for you, My sheep, the sheep of My pasture, you are men, and I am your God," declares the Lord God.

—Ezekiel 34:27, 30–31

What will Israel know and when will they know?

Specifically what will they know about God? How are the people described?

While there were faithful shepherds and followers in Ezekiel's day, there were even more who were not. We see the similarity in the church today. There are faithful leaders and followers, but many have left the true path of the Word of God. Nevertheless, God remains faithful. His mercies are new every morning and His faithfulness is great (Lam. 3:23). As you consider what you have studied today, read the verse below and express what is in your heart.

O Lord, You are my God; I will exalt You, I will give thanks to Your name; For You have worked wonders, Plans formed long ago, with perfect faithfulness.

Isaiah 25:1

Chapter Eighteen

FREEDOM PROMISED

Luke 4:18–21 is the fulfillment of Isaiah 61:1.

The Spirit of the Lord God is upon me, because the Lord has anointed me to bring good news to the afflicted; He has sent me to bind up the brokenhearted, to proclaim liberty to captives And freedom to prisoners.

—Isaiah 61:1

"The Spirit of the Lord is upon me, because he anointed me to preach the gospel the poor. He has sent me to proclaim release to the captives, and recovery of sight to the blind, to set free those who are oppressed, to proclaim the favorable year of the Lord." And He closed the book, gave it back to the attendant and sat down; and the eyes of all in the synagogue were fixed on Him. And He began to say to them, "Today this Scripture has been fulfilled in your hearing."

—Luke 4:18–20

Compare the two passages and note what Jesus was sent to do. For example:

Isaiah 61:1   **Luke 4:18**
a. Bring good news   Preach the gospel
b. Bind up   Proclaim release

c.
d.

Reread Luke 4:18 and Isaiah 61:1. In the space below, record who Jesus would help? Be specific.

Isaiah calls the people afflicted and brokenhearted, captives and prisoners. Luke calls them the poor, captives, blind, and oppressed. Let's look at some definitions. Hebrew is the language used in the Old Testament, and Greek is used in the New Testament.

WORD STUDY

Afflicted or poor—Hebrew is *anau*, Greek is *ptochos,* meaning, "depressed in mind or circumstance."

Brokenhearted—Hebrew is *shavar,* meaning those whose hearts/minds are subject "to burst, break in pieces, to crush, to smash, to be maimed." Greek is *suntribo kardia,* meaning "to crush, shatter the seat, center of life (thoughts, feelings, mind)" of individuals.

Captives—Hebrew word is *shavah,* meaning those who are "to be led away, to be held captive." The main idea is that of a military force subduing their enemies and taking them as prisoners. The Greek is *aichmalotos,* meaning "those taken by the sword, a captive, those who have become captives of the devil."

Prisoners—Hebrew is *acar,* meaning those who are bound or "yoked, fastened; hold, in prison."

Oppressed—Greek is *thrauo,* meaning, "broken in pieces, crushed, bruised, oppressed." In the New Testament, "crushing the strength of someone."

Blind—Greek is *tuflov*, "unable to see clearly." Figuratively, refers to being ignorant, stupid, slow of understanding.

What kind of people will Jesus help? Those who have been crushed, broken, maimed in their thoughts or feelings. He will help those led away captive, subdued, taken by sword, held captive by the devil. He will help those who are yoked or bruised, those whose strength has been crushed and those who cannot see clearly in respect to the mind and understanding.

Who would this include? Anyone in any bondage anywhere! People in chains, in prison; anywhere there is a battle for the mind; anyone who is in physical, mental, emotional, intellectual, psychological, moral, or spiritual bondage, people who are being manipulated, those who want to be free, those who think they cannot be free, even those who don't want to be free. God has called us to live in freedom and to tell this world about Him.

Can you see yourself or someone you know in that list now or sometime in the past? If so, in what area? Does the bondage still exist?

Can you also see the help available in Jesus? Write it out below.

What kind of help will He provide? Isaiah says He will proclaim liberty and freedom. Luke says He will preach the gospel, release captives, recover sight to the blind, and set people free.

WORD STUDY

The Hebrew word for "preach good news" is *basar*, meaning "to bring, carry, publish." The Greek is *euaggelizo*, meaning "to announce good news, especially the gospel. bring, show."

"Bind up" in Hebrew is *chabash*, meaning "to heal, to wrap up, compress."

"Heal" in Greek is *iáomai*, meaning "to heal, cure, restore to bodily health." Can be used metaphorically, referring to moral diseases, as in "to save from the consequences of sin."

"Recovery of sight" in Greek is *anablepsis*, meaning "restoration of sight."

"Liberty" in Hebrew is *darowr*, meaning "freedom, spontaneous outflow."

"Deliverance" in Greek is *aphesis*, meaning one who has been released or "to cause to stand away, to release one's sins from the sinner." In Isaiah 61:1 and Luke 4:18, man is presented as *aichmálotos*, a prisoner of war, a captive. *Áphesis* involves the new birth of man spiritually or in his inner self (John 3:1–12). *Áphesis* does not involve simply the freedom of the sinner, but the change of the sinner from being a slave of sin to becoming a slave of God.

Christ preached the good news (the gospel, the power of God for salvation). He healed broken hearts; He restored moral health; He saved people from the consequences of sin; He restored sight and understanding. He provided freedom from sin and the ability to have a spontaneous outflow, a freedom of action, freedom from sin and toward God. He provided deliverance from everything that held man a prisoner away from God. He does not simply take man out of prison, he changes him radically, giving him power over sin and the ability to live holy on a consistent basis.

> Giving thanks unto the Father, which hath made us meet to be partakers of the inheritance of the saints in light: Who hath delivered us from the power of darkness, and hath translated us into the kingdom of his dear Son.
> —Colossians 1:12–13 (KJV)

Christ broke the yoke of bondage—every bondage, any bondage, all bondage. According to Colossians 1:12–13, what else did the Father do?

The yoke has been broken and the chains removed; thus freedom rings. Do you know of someone who needs this truth, someone who can be set free today? Perhaps an unbeliever who does not know Jesus or a believer who is not living in the freedom Christ has provided for His own. Will you tell someone about the freedom that Christ provides?

What about you? Are you living in all the freedom that Christ has provided? Don't let anyone or anything keep you from the freedom that has been provided for you. How the spirit of God must be grieved when, after all He has done for us in Christ, we still walk around in chains of bondage. God sent Moses to Pharaoh to tell him, ***"Let My people go."***

Bondage is not knowing what freedom you have. Bondage also means not living in the freedom you could have. Ask God to give you the courage to live free every day and the boldness to give His freedom to others.

Chapter Nineteen

WHAT HE DID

Read the following verses and record your answers from the text.

Therefore, since the children share in flesh and blood, He Himself likewise also partook of the same, that through death He might render powerless him who had the power of death, that is, the devil, and might free those who through fear of death were subject to slavery all their lives.
—Hebrews 2:14–15

What did Christ do and to whom? Who was freed?

The one who practices sin is of the devil; for the devil has sinned from the beginning. The Son of God appeared for this purpose, to destroy the works of the devil. No one who is born of God practices sin, because His seed abides in him; and he cannot sin, because he is born of God.
—1 John 3:8–9

Record what Christ did and to whom. What difference does that make to you?

Look at the word *cannot* in verse 9.

WORD STUDY

The Greek word for "can" is *dunamai*, meaning "of uncertain affinity; to be able or possible:–be able, can (do, + -not), could, may, might, be possible, be of power."
The Greek word for "not" is *ou*, meaning "an absolute negative; nay, neither, never, no."

The combined meaning is "does not have the ability or power to." The verse is saying that the one born of God does not have the power or ability to keep sinning because Jesus destroyed the works of Satan. Jesus' seed is in the one born of Him.

> He made Him who knew no sin to be sin on our behalf, so that we might become the righteousness of God in Him.
> —2 Corinthians 5:21

Record what Christ did. What was the result?

> Grace to you and peace from God our Father and the Lord Jesus Christ, who gave Himself for our sins so that He might rescue us from this present evil age, according to the will of our God and Father.
> —Galatians 1:3–4

What did Christ do? What were we rescued from?

What He Did

WORD STUDY

The Greek word for "age" is *aion*, meaning "by implication, the world; age, course, eternal, (for) ever."

May it never be! How shall we who died to sin still live in it? Or do you not know that all of us who have been baptized into Christ Jesus have been baptized into His death? knowing this, that our old self was crucified with Him, in order that our body of sin might be done away with, so that we would no longer be slaves to sin; for he who has died is freed from sin.
—Romans 6:2–7

What did He do? What was the result?

For the grace of God has appeared, bringing salvation to all men, instructing us to deny ungodliness and worldly desires and to live sensibly, righteously and godly in the present age, looking for the blessed hope and the appearing of the glory of our great God and Savior, Christ Jesus, who gave Himself for us to redeem us from every lawless deed, and to purify for Himself a people for His own possession, zealous for good deeds.
—Titus 2:11–14

What did He do? What was the result?

How much more will the blood of Christ, who through the eternal Spirit offered Himself without blemish to God, cleanse your conscience from dead works to serve the living God?
—Hebrews 9:14

What did He do? What was the result?

But you are a chosen race, a royal priesthood, a holy nation, a people for God's own possession, so that you may proclaim the excellencies of Him who has called you out of darkness into His marvelous light; for you once were not a people, but now you are the people of God; you had not received mercy, but now you have received mercy.

—1 Peter 2:9–10

What did He do? What was the result? What are they now called? What were they called before? What did they receive?

For we also once were foolish ourselves, disobedient, deceived, enslaved to various lusts and pleasures, spending our life in malice and envy, hateful, hating one another. But when the kindness of God our Savior and His love for mankind appeared, He saved us, not on the basis of deeds which we have done in righteousness, but according to His mercy, by the washing of regeneration and renewing by the Holy Spirit, whom He poured out upon us richly through Jesus Christ our Savior, so that being justified by His grace we would be made heirs according to the hope of eternal life.

—Titus 3:3–7

What did He do? What was the result? List the before and after.

But God, being rich in mercy, because of His great love with which He loved us, even when we were dead in our transgressions, made us alive together with Christ (by grace you have been saved), and raised us up with Him, and seated us with Him in the heavenly places in Christ Jesus, For we are His workmanship, created in Christ Jesus for good works, which God prepared beforehand so that we would walk in them.

—Ephesians 2:4–10

What He Did

What did He do? What was the result?

Jesus freed us from the guilt and power of sin, from the power of the world, and from the power of Satan. He took us from being deceived and enslaved to being heirs in His kingdom. He made us His own possession, called us holy, royal, peculiar, and gave us the ability to consistently live for Him, zealously doing good works. He even prepared our assigned work beforehand and called them "good works." He did all this and much more. You can read the rest of the story in His Book.

After all you have learned today, consider what God would have you do with this amazing truth about Christ and what He has done for you. Since He died to make all this happen for you, are you willing to live so that it will? Write out changes you need to make so that the freedom that Christ has provided for you will be evident in your life.

Chapter Twenty

THE BONDAGE—BROKEN

Mia, a friend and Bible student, told me of how God broke the bondage in her life. This is her story: She was sixteen, pregnant, and had been raised a Catholic. Her Catholic father took her to New York for an abortion because it was not legal in Ohio. She'd grown up in Catholic schools, loved God, and was grateful to Jesus and Mary. For several years she wanted to be a nun. Obviously that goal did not last.

After the abortion, the Catholic practice of excommunication seemed appropriate to her. She had committed murder, which was considered a mortal sin, so according to the rules she should be thrown out of the church.

From that day forward, she behaved like the fallen creature she knew she was. She was sexually promiscuous all through college, but eventually married her childhood sweetheart, a man she had dated when she was sixteen. That first year of marriage was a war zone. So when she found herself pregnant, they agreed she should have another abortion. Over the next nineteen years of marriage, she had five brief affairs.

How does someone go from years in a religious atmosphere to sexual promiscuity? Don't all those classes and sermons mean something?

When you feel like trash, you tend to live like trash. As long as you can get along in society and make a good living, does anybody really care? When the situation looks hopeless, who can you run to?

Mia is not alone and her feelings are not new. Look at Job.

> Where now is my hope? And who regards my hope?
>
> —Job 17:15

Obviously, there is hope. That hope is in Jesus. He came to seek and save the lost, to bring good news to the afflicted. He came to bind up the brokenhearted, to proclaim liberty to the captives and freedom to the prisoners. Whatever your bondage may be, Jesus is your liberator. If you are not saved, turn now to the appendix (God's plan for salvation) and see how you can be set free and live free.

Mia finally took advantage of the freedom Jesus offers. She became a Christian before the last two affairs, but kept that part of her life compartmentalized. She thought Jesus saved her and wouldn't notice her sin. But after she spent time studying the Word of God, He turned the magnifying glass on that area of her life. She accepted the freedom Christ provided, releasing her from bondage.

John 8 tells the story of another woman God turned the magnifying glass on.

> Early in the morning He came again into the temple, and all the people were coming to Him; and He sat down and began to teach them. The scribes and the Pharisees brought a woman caught in adultery, and having set her in the center of the court, they said to Him, "Teacher, this woman has been caught in adultery, in the very act."
>
> —John 8:2–4

What time is it? Where is Jesus and what is He doing? Who is there? What is the issue?

> "Now in the Law Moses commanded us to stone such women; what then do You say?" They were saying this, testing Him, so that they might have grounds for accusing Him. But Jesus stooped down and with His finger wrote on the ground.
>
> —John 8:5–6

The Bondage—Broken

The scribes and Pharisees knew the Law said to stone this woman. What they do not mention is that the Law says to stone both the man and the woman (Deuteronomy 22:22). The Law also required more than one witness. Reread verse 5–6 and record what they are really doing here.

She is obviously guilty, having been "caught in the act." Did she even have time to dress? She faces certain death. But the issue is not really about her. No one seems to be concerned about what happens to this woman. Can you imagine her standing there in front of all those people, early in the morning, with little or no clothing on? What started as a passionate tryst with a forbidden lover turned into a public trial, with no lover in sight—or so she thought. What shame she must have been experiencing, a labeled adulteress and now a tool to be used to trap Jesus.

Jesus' response is not what anyone would have predicted. He simply writes on the ground.

> But when they persisted in asking Him, He straightened up, and said to them, "He who is without sin among you, let him be the first to throw a stone at her." Again He stooped down and wrote on the ground.
>
> —John 8:7–8

How quickly the tables turn when Jesus brings the woman back into the picture. The trap the religious leaders set for Jesus becomes their own. What did Jesus write? We don't know. But whatever He said drove His point home. Write out what Jesus said to them.

> When they heard it, they began to go out one by one, beginning with the older ones, and He was left alone, and the woman, where she was, in the center of the court.
>
> —John 8:9

You can almost hear the stones drop. They did not run off, they just slipped away one by one. The older, "wiser" guys left first, then the younger. Then what? Record below who is left.

> Straightening up, Jesus said to her, "Woman, where are they? Did no one condemn you?" She said, "No one, Lord." And Jesus said, "I do not condemn you, either. Go. From now on sin no more."
>
> —John 8:10–11

Jesus knows she is guilty, but He does not accuse her. He does not give her a sermon, and He does not throw a stone. What does He ask her? What is His comment and command to her?

WORD STUDY

The Greek word for "condemn" is *katakrino*, meaning "to judge against; i.e., sentence:–condemn, damn. To pronounce sentence against, condemn, adjudge guilty."

"Go" and "sin no more" are both present imperatives, which means she was commanded to go, and from that point on sin was not to be repeated or continued.

Jesus knows she is guilty, but He does not condemn her or judge her. He does not count her sin against her. (Just like what happens to our sins at salvation.) He tells her to go and not repeat or continue in sin. She started the day with one lover, but ended up with the lover of her soul, Jesus Christ. She started out with sin, but ended up with a pardon. She should have had death, but ended up with life.

Read verses 10–11 again. What does the woman call Jesus? Record that here.

The Bondage—Broken

Want to know the rest of Mia's story? This is how the Lord set her free.

God brought about circumstances that forced her to confess her sins to her husband. She no longer wanted to be married, especially under false pretenses. So she confessed everything to him so he could make a decision about whether to stay married to her. Dredging up the truth about her marital affairs was cleansing for her, yet she still felt dirty, unworthy, and defeated.

To her extreme shock, her husband decided to stay with her. Even though he said it was for the sake of the kids, the Lord showed her how much her husband really loved her.

After confession came repentance. She renounced that sin and gave it no place in her life. She memorized a Scripture verse and repeated it every time temptation tried to enter her thoughts. "I will take every thought captive and make it obedient to Christ" (2 Corinthians 10:5). She was using "the sword of the spirit," (Ephesians 6:17) as Jesus did when He was tempted in the wilderness (Matthew 4:1).

At first the temptations were plentiful. But it helped her to know that temptation did not mean she was still in bondage. She learned firsthand that if you "resist the devil…he will flee from you" (James 4:7).

She is now truly a new creature in Christ. He has completely excised that part of her and she is free—free to serve and free to love. He has shown her who she is in Christ. He has forgiven all her trespasses and put them as far as the east is from the west. She admits that Satan occasionally fills her with regret for the wasteful and destructive life she has led. But God always assures her He will use even that for good.

She started out with sin (don't we all?) but ended up with a pardon. She should have had death, but received eternal life. She found the lover of her soul, Jesus Christ.

Your Assignment: "Take The Yoke"

Chapter Twenty-One
───────────────

So What's the Problem?

Since Christ has done such a magnificent work, why are so many people still in bondage?

> Come to Me, all who are weary and heavy-laden, and I will give you rest. Take My yoke upon you and learn from Me, for I am gentle and humble in heart, and you will find rest for your souls. For My yoke is easy and My burden is light.
>
> —Matthew 11:28–30

What is Jesus offering? How does He describe Himself? Who is He asking to come? What must they do once the yoke is taken? Will it be difficult?

WORD STUDY

The Greek word for "yoke" in this passage is *zugos*, meaning, "serving to couple any two things together." In the New Testament, it denotes "severe precepts, the precepts of Christ; a coupling; pair of balances."

The Greek word for "learn" is *manthano*, meaning "to learn (in any way):–learn, understand."

The Greek word for "rest" is *anapausis*, meaning "intermission; by implication, recreation:–rest."

The Greek word for "burden" is *phortion*, used in the New Testament only figuratively, as the burden of Christ's commandments (Matthew 11:30).

Jesus promises to give rest to the weary and heavy-laden. Rest comes when the yoke is taken. Since yoke means two things coupled together, the two things coupled together are (1) Jesus (learning from Jesus) and (2) anyone who comes to Him and takes the yoke. Those who come to Him will learn of Him since He is in them seeking after Himself.

The soul will rest, or take intermission, as the learning goes on. His yoke (the coupling) will be easy and the burden (or commandments) will be light because He is shouldering the weight. Taking Jesus' yoke means freedom!

Read the following passage and note what you see about the gospel.

> For I am not ashamed of the gospel, for it is the power of God for salvation to everyone who believes, to the Jew first and also to the Greek. For in it the righteousness of God is revealed from faith to faith; as it is written, "But the righteous man shall live by faith."
> —Romans 1:16–17

The gospel is…

According to this passage, for whom is the gospel written? How are they described?

So What's the Problem?

Do you recall the definition for belief we discussed in Chapter 15? You may want to review it again. Basically, it is a firm persuasion that results in a transformation of character and way of life. After salvation the person is considered righteous. According to Romans 1:16–17, how then must that person live?

Where does belief (faith) come in, for salvation or after salvation? Can you see the potential bondage situations for those with and without salvation? Why?

Read the following passages, circling the word *believe* (*believes, belief,* etc.), and record what happens to those who do or do not believe.

> For God so loved the world, that He gave His only begotten Son, that whoever believes in Him shall not perish, but have eternal life. For God did not send the Son into the world to judge the world, but that the world might be saved through Him. He who believes in Him is not judged; he who does not believe has been judged already, because he has not believed in the name of the only begotten Son of God.
>
> —John 3:16–18

> Therefore I said to you that you will die in your sins; for unless you believe that I am He, you will die in your sins.
>
> —John 8:24

And with whom was He angry for forty years? Was it not with those who sinned, whose bodies fell in the wilderness? And to whom did He swear that they would not enter His rest, but to those who were disobedient? So we see that they were not able to enter because of unbelief.

—Hebrews 3:17–19

Why couldn't they enter His rest? Look for two reasons.

As you continue to read, mark *faith*. *Faith* (the noun) and *believe* (the verb) have the same root meaning.

And without faith it is impossible to please Him, for he who comes to God must believe that He is and that He is a rewarder of those who seek Him.

—Hebrews 11:6

And He said to them, "Because of the littleness of your faith; for truly I say to you, if you have faith the size of a mustard seed, you will say to this mountain, 'Move from here to there,' and it will move; and nothing will be impossible to you."

—Matthew 17:20

And all things you ask in prayer, believing, you will receive.

—Matthew 21:22

So What's the Problem?

> He has now reconciled you in His fleshly body through death, in order to present you before Him holy and blameless and beyond reproach—if indeed you continue in the faith firmly established and steadfast, and not moved away from the hope of the gospel that you have heard, which was proclaimed in all creation under heaven, and of which I, Paul, was made a minister.
> —Colossians 1:22–23

> Therefore as you have received Christ Jesus the Lord, so walk in Him, having been firmly rooted and now being built up in Him and established in your faith, just as you were instructed, and overflowing with gratitude. See to it that no one takes you captive through philosophy and empty deception, according to the tradition of men, according to the elementary principles of the world, rather than according to Christ.
> —Colossians 2:6–8

When we were studying John 8 (Chapter 16) we learned that knowing the truth shall make us free. Now, if truth makes us free, what do faith, belief, or unbelief have to do with it? Is knowing the truth enough?

Your thoughts:

> But are you willing to recognize, you foolish fellow, that faith without works is useless? Was not Abraham our father justified by works when he offered up Isaac his son on the altar? You see that faith was working with his works, and as a result of the works, faith was perfected.
> —James 2:20–22

Was Abraham free or in bondage when He offered up Isaac? Why?

Read Genesis 22, marking *Abraham* and *God*.

> Now it came about after these things, that God tested Abraham, and said to him, "Abraham!" And he said, "Here I am." He said, "Take now your son, your only son, whom you love, Isaac, and go to the land of Moriah, and offer him there as a burnt offering on one of the mountains of which I will tell you." So Abraham rose early in the morning and saddled his donkey, and took two of his young men with him and Isaac his son; and he split wood for the burnt offering, and arose and went to the place of which God had told him.
>
> On the third day Abraham raised his eyes and saw the place from a distance. Abraham said to his young men, "Stay here with the donkey, and I and the lad will go over there; and we will worship and return to you." Abraham took the wood of the burnt offering and laid it on Isaac his son, and he took in his hand the fire and the knife. So the two of them walked on together.
>
> Isaac spoke to Abraham his father and said, "My father!" And he said, "Here I am, my son." And he said, "Behold, the fire and the wood, but where is the lamb for the burnt offering?" Abraham said, "God will provide for Himself the lamb for the burnt offering, my son." So the two of them walked on together.
>
> Then they came to the place of which God had told him; and Abraham built the altar there and arranged the wood, and bound his son Isaac and laid him on the altar, on top of the wood. Abraham stretched out his hand and took the knife to slay his son. But the angel of the Lord called to him from heaven and said, "Abraham, Abraham!" And he said, "Here I am." He said, "Do not stretch out your hand against the lad, and do nothing to him; for now I know that you fear God, since you have not withheld your son, your only son, from Me." Then Abraham raised his eyes and looked, and behold, behind him a ram caught in the thicket by his horns; and Abraham went and took the ram and offered him up for a burnt offering in the place of his son.

So What's the Problem?

Abraham called the name of that place The Lord Will Provide, as it is said to this day, "In the mount of the Lord it will be provided." Then the angel of the Lord called to Abraham a second time from heaven, and said, "By Myself I have sworn, declares the Lord, because you have done this thing and have not withheld your son, your only son, indeed I will greatly bless you, and I will greatly multiply your seed as the stars of the heavens and as the sand which is on the seashore; and your seed shall possess the gate of their enemies. "In your seed all the nations of the earth shall be blessed, because you have obeyed My voice."

—Genesis 22:1–18

What was God doing with Abraham?

What was Abraham's attitude?

How could he be so confident? Was he free or in bondage? Was this really faith?

By faith Abraham, when he was tested, offered up Isaac, and he who had received the promises was offering up his only begotten son; it was he to whom it was said, "In Isaac your descendants shall be called." He considered that God is able to raise people even from the dead, from which he also received him back as a type.

—Hebrews 11:17–19

What was the basis of his faith according to this passage? Was he free or in bondage?

God's promise is His word, and because Abraham believed God's word, according to James 2:22, his faith moved into action.

> For this reason we also constantly thank God that when you received the word of God which you heard from us, you accepted it not as the word of men, but for what it really is, the word of God, which also performs its work in you who believe.
> —1 Thessalonians 2:13

When will the Word perform its work in you? Write out your answer.

The truth shall make you free! Believers are free to move in what God has said in His Word—free to live holy and to move in His blessings.

If there is a yoke in your life that is not broken, remember that Christ has done His part. Could it be that the yoke is not broken because you do not really believe the Word in that area? You believe for salvation, but what about other things? Unbelief will keep a sinner out of heaven; it will also keep a believer from experiencing all the blessings of God.

Chapter Twenty-Two

They Had It But Didn't Get It

Imagine living in your father's house, enjoying all that he has provided for you: food, the car, a charge card, every luxury within the limits of his rule. Then you tire of it and decide to take your share, leave your father's house, and do what you want with all the provisions your father has given you.

Jesus told the following parable:

"A man had two sons. The younger of them said to his father, 'Father, give me the share of the estate that falls to me.' So he divided his wealth between them. And not many days later, the younger son gathered everything together and went on a journey into a distant country, and there he squandered his estate with loose living. Now when he had spent everything, a severe famine occurred in that country, and he began to be impoverished. So he went and hired himself out to one of the citizens of that country, and he sent him into his fields to feed swine. And he would have gladly filled his stomach with the pods that the swine were eating, and no one was giving anything to him."

—Luke 15:11–16

What was the young man's request? How did the father respond? How did the son handle his share? What was the young man's condition after he ran out of money?

"But when he came to his senses, he said, 'How many of my father's hired men have more than enough bread, but I am dying here with hunger! I will get up and go to my father, and will say to him, "Father, I have sinned against heaven, and in your sight; I am no longer worthy to be called your son; make me as one of your hired men."'"

—Luke 15:17–19

What did the son finally come to (verse 17)? What was he willing to admit? What was he willing to accept?

"So he got up and came to his father. But while he was still a long way off, his father saw him and felt compassion for him, and ran and embraced him and kissed him. And the son said to him, 'Father, I have sinned against heaven and in your sight; I am no longer worthy to be called your son.' But the father said to his slaves, 'Quickly bring out the best robe and put it on him, and put a ring on his hand and sandals on his feet; and bring the fattened calf, kill it, and let us eat and celebrate; for this son of mine was dead and has come to life again; he was lost and has been found.' And they began to celebrate."

—Luke 15:20–24

Make a list of the father's responses. How does he describe his son?

They Had It But Didn't Get It

Think of all the father's blessings that the son had at home and left behind. Think about what he experienced when he left. Think of all he did not receive while he was "out there." And think about all that he missed and would never receive because the opportunity had passed.

Is there anything he had after he came back home that he did not have before he left? What does he have now that he could not see before he left? All that the father had, he still has, all that the son has access to, he still has. Has anything really changed?

> "Now his older son was in the field, and when he came and approached the house, he heard music and dancing. And he summoned one of the servants and began inquiring what these things could be. And he said to him, 'Your brother has come, and your father has killed the fattened calf because he has received him back safe and sound.' But he became angry and was not willing to go in; and his father came out and began pleading with him. But he answered and said to his father, 'Look! For so many years I have been serving you and I have never neglected a command of yours; and yet you have never given me a young goat, so that I might celebrate with my friends; but when this son of yours came, who has devoured your wealth with prostitutes, you killed the fattened calf for him.' And he said to him, 'Son, you have always been with me, and all that is mine is yours. But we had to celebrate and rejoice, for this brother of yours was dead and has begun to live, and was lost and has been found.'"
>
> —Luke 15:25–32

Why is the elder son so angry? What does he have that he cannot seem to see? Can he learn a lesson from the younger son?

As children of our heavenly Father, we have access to all that He has. Is there anything He has that you cannot see that you have access to?

So then let no one boast in men. For all things belong to you, whether Paul or Apollos or Cephas or the world or life or death or things present or things to come; all things belong to you, and you belong to Christ; and Christ belongs to God.

—1 Corinthians 3:21–23

To whom do you belong? What belongs to you? Will you walk in what the Father has provided to you through the Son? It is all there. Christ has set you free. Will you live in the freedom He has provided?

Chapter Twenty-Three
────────────────

A Made-up Mind

Jesus went away from there, and withdrew into the district of Tyre and Sidon. And a Canaanite woman from that region came out and began to cry out, saying, "Have mercy on me, Lord, Son of David; my daughter is cruelly demon-possessed."

—Matthew 15:21–22

Note all that you see about the woman: who she is, where she is from, and what she knows about Jesus. What is her concern? What does she call Jesus? What is her request?

But He did not answer her a word. And His disciples came and implored Him, saying, "Send her away, because she keeps shouting at us."
—Matthew 15:23

How does Jesus respond to her concern? How do the disciples respond?

Would you have been discouraged if Jesus had not answered you? Would you have allowed other people to dissuade you?

Truth will set you free when it is applied. What does she know about Jesus?

But He answered and said, "I was sent only to the lost sheep of the house of Israel."
—Matthew 15:24

What does this answer mean to the woman? Is she an Israelite?

But she came and began to bow down before Him, saying, "Lord, help me!"
—Matthew 15:25

A Made-up Mind

WORD STUDY

The Greek word for "bow" is *proskunéo*, meaning "to kiss, adore; to worship, do obeisance, show respect, fall or prostrate before. Literally, to kiss toward someone, to throw a kiss in token of respect or homage." In the New Testament, it means "to do reverence or homage to someone, usually by kneeling or prostrating oneself before him." The Greek construction here is that she repeatedly says, "Lord, help me." Help is present imperative active, which means it is continuous, repeated action and it is a command.

Jesus would not answer this woman, and the disciples wanted to send her away. Jesus even excludes her by saying He has come to the lost sheep of the house of Israel. She has essentially been rejected three times, yet she worships Him.

We often think of worship as expressing thanks for something that has been done. After He touches you, after He moves in your life, after the healing, after the financial blessing, after being kept in safety, you know you will never be the same. It is a voluntary act of gratitude for something. But this lady has received nothing but rejections, and yet she worships. Her worship is based on who He is, what He has done, and what she believes He can do.

Reread verse 22 and record the type of help she needs and wants from Jesus. Also record what she calls Him.

> And He answered and said, "It is not good to take the children's bread and throw it to the dogs."
>
> —Matthew 15:26

Rejection number four! Record it.

This woman is a Canaanite woman, a Gentile. Gentiles were generally referred to as dogs. Who are the children? Reread verse 24. What is the implication?

But she said, "Yes, Lord; but even the dogs feed on the crumbs which fall from their masters' table."

—Matthew 15:27

What is the woman suggesting? How can she be so insistent about getting what she wants? Notice what she calls Jesus.

She does not want what belongs to someone else, but what belongs to her. From verse 22, what is her request? What does she know Jesus can do?

Then Jesus said to her, "O woman, your faith is great; it shall be done for you as you wish." And her daughter was healed at once.

—Matthew 15:28

Jesus calls her faith great. From the seven verses we have studied about this woman, list reasons Jesus would have called her faith great.

How could she keep her focus in light of all the rejections? Could it be what she knew about Jesus and what she believed He could do (verse 22)? This is a lady who refused to accept the bondage. She moved to the One who could handle her problem, and she refused to let go until she was blessed.

What did she have to give up before Jesus healed her daughter? How long did it take for the daughter to be healed? Is there anything you are holding on to that is in the way of your freedom? Are you willing to give it up?

How quickly can God respond when you give it up? How great is your faith? God says, **"Let My people go."** So let go!

Why God Allows It

Chapter Twenty-Four
_____

PURPOSE PLANNED

Have you ever asked God, "Why me? Why is this happening to me? Why is this so hard?" Let's go back and look at some of the individuals we have already studied and see if we can find any reasons.

Joseph (from chapter 5). Why was Joseph in bondage? What was God's plan and purpose? Joseph responded well, but so what? Why did God put him through such rigorous training?

Read Genesis 45:5–7 and record any reason you may see for the bondage.

> Now do not be grieved or angry with yourselves, because you sold me here, for God sent me before you to preserve life. For the famine has been in the land these two years, and there are still five years in which there will be neither plowing nor harvesting. God sent me before you to preserve for you a remnant in the earth, and to keep you alive by a great deliverance.
> —Genesis 45:5–7

Read Genesis 50:19–21 and record any reason you see for the bondage.

But Joseph said to them, "Do not be afraid, for am I in God's place? As for you, you meant evil against me, but God meant it for good in order to bring about this present result, to preserve many people alive. So therefore, do not be afraid; I will provide for you and your little ones." So he comforted them and spoke kindly to them.

—Genesis 50:19–21

The Israelites in Egypt (from chapter 6)
Read the following Scriptures and record any reasons you may see for the bondage.

"Say, therefore, to the sons of Israel, 'I am the Lord, and I will bring you out from under the burdens of the Egyptians, and I will deliver you from their bondage. I will also redeem you with an outstretched arm and with great judgments. Then I will take you for My people, and I will be your God; and you shall know that I am the Lord your God, who brought you out from under the burdens of the Egyptians.'"

—Exodus 6:6–7

The Egyptians shall know that I am the Lord, when I stretch out My hand on Egypt and bring out the sons of Israel from their midst.

—Exodus 7:5

Then the Lord said to Moses, "Rise up early in the morning and stand before Pharaoh and say to him, 'Thus says the Lord, the God of the Hebrews, "Let My people go, that they may serve Me. For this time I will send all My plagues on you and your servants and your people, so that you may know that there is no one like Me in all the earth. For if by now I had put forth My hand and struck you and your people with pestilence, you would then have been cut off from the earth. But, indeed, for this reason I have allowed you to remain, in order to show you My power and in order to proclaim My name through all the earth."

—Exodus 9:13–16

Purpose Planned

The Israelites in Isaiah (from chapter 9). Let's look for a reason for the bondage. Record what you see under each passage.

"Woe to the rebellious children," declares the Lord, "who execute a plan, but not Mine, And make an alliance, but not of My Spirit, In order to add sin to sin."
—Isaiah 30:1

Therefore thus says the Holy One of Israel, "Since you have rejected this word and have put your trust in oppression and guile, and have relied on them, therefore this iniquity will be to you like a breach about to fall, a bulge in a high wall, whose collapse comes suddenly in an instant."
—Isaiah 30:12–13

For thus the Lord GOD, the Holy One of Israel, has said, "In repentance and rest you will be saved, In quietness and trust is your strength." But you were not willing.
—Isaiah 30:15

God gives them a way out. What is their response?

Woe to those who deeply hide their plans from the Lord, and whose deeds are done in a dark place, and they say, "Who sees us?" or "Who knows us?" You turn things around! Shall the potter be considered as equal with the clay, that what is made would say to its maker, "He did not make me"; or what is formed say to him who formed it, "He has no understanding"?
—Isaiah 29:15–16

How did Israel view God?

Job (from chapter 10). Is there a reason for Job's bondage?

Then Job arose and tore his robe and shaved his head, and he fell to the ground and worshiped. He said, "Naked I came from my mother's womb, And naked I shall return there. The Lord gave and the Lord has taken away. Blessed be the name of the Lord." Through all this Job did not sin nor did he blame God.

—Job 1:20–22

What is Job's response?

But he said to her, "You speak as one of the foolish women speaks. Shall we indeed accept good from God and not accept adversity?" In all this Job did not sin with his lips.

—Job 2:10

Record Job's response.

Though he slay me, yet will I trust in him: but I will maintain mine own ways before him.

—Job 13:15 (KJV)

Record Job's response.

WORD STUDY

The Hebrew for "maintain" is *yakach*, meaning "to prove, to argue, convince, maintain, plead, reason (together)."

Then Job answered the Lord and said, "I know that You can do all things, and that no purpose of Yours can be thwarted. 'Who is this that hides counsel without knowledge?' Therefore I have declared that which I did not understand, things too wonderful for me, which I did not know. 'Hear, now, and I will speak; I will ask You, and You instruct me.' I have heard of You by the hearing of the ear; but now my eye sees You; therefore I retract, And I repent in dust and ashes." It came about after the Lord had spoken these words to Job, that the Lord said to Eliphaz the

Purpose Planned

Temanite, "My wrath is kindled against you and against your two friends, because you have not spoken of Me what is right as My servant Job has."

—Job 42:1–7

What does Job admit in verse 5?

David (from chapter 13). Record any reason you see for this bondage. Below is the Psalm David wrote after his affair with Bathsheba.

Be gracious to me, O God, according to Your lovingkindness; According to the greatness of Your compassion blot out my transgressions. Wash me thoroughly from my iniquity And cleanse me from my sin. For I know my transgressions, And my sin is ever before me.

—Psalm 51:1–3

Do you recall the definitions for the three words for sin that David uses here?

Create in me a clean heart, O God, And renew a steadfast spirit within me. Do not cast me away from Your presence And do not take Your Holy Spirit from me. Restore to me the joy of Your salvation And sustain me with a willing spirit. Then I will teach transgressors Your ways, And sinners will be converted to You. Deliver me from bloodguiltiness, O God, the God of my salvation; Then my tongue will joyfully sing of Your righteousness. O Lord, open my lips, That my mouth may declare Your praise.

—Psalm 51:10–15

Once David acknowledges his sin, what does he ask God to do? What does he promise God he will do? What result does David mention?

Read the following verse and record what David knew about his purpose.

> And David realized that the Lord had established him as king over Israel, and that He had exalted his kingdom for the sake of His people Israel.
>
> —2 Samuel 5:12

Summarize the reasons for bondage that you have found by studying Scriptures about:

a. Joseph:

b. The Israelites in Egypt:

c. The Israelites in Isaiah:

d. Job:

e. David:

Do you see any common ground among the five examples above?

Chapter Twenty-Five
___

POTENTIAL PERFECTED

As we continue to consider why God allows bondage, we will review a few passages from the New Testament. We can obviously see sin, but we can also see God working all things together for the good of those who are the called according to His purpose (Romans 8:28).

Read the following passages, recording any reason you may see for the bondage.

Example #1 - From Jesus in the Sermon on the Mount

Blessed are you when people insult you and persecute you, and falsely say all kinds of evil against you because of Me. Rejoice and be glad, for your reward in heaven is great; for in the same way they persecuted the prophets who were before you. You are the salt of the earth; but if the salt has become tasteless, how can it be made salty again? It is no longer good for anything, except to be thrown out and trampled under foot by men. You are the light of the world. A city set on a hill cannot be hidden; nor does anyone light a lamp and put it under a basket, but on the lampstand, and it gives light to all who are in the house. Let your light shine before men in such a way that they may see your good works, and glorify your Father who is in heaven.

—Matthew 5:11–16

Notice who is blessed and the response. Record also what they are told to do.

Example #2 - From John recording how Jesus healed a blind man

As He passed by, He saw a man blind from birth. And His disciples asked Him, "Rabbi, who sinned, this man or his parents, that he would be born blind?" Jesus answered, "It was neither that this man sinned, nor his parents; but it was so that the works of God might be displayed in him."

—John 9:1–3

Here we see a different kind of bondage. What is the reason for the blindness?

Example #3 - From Paul to Timothy

Remember Jesus Christ, risen from the dead, descendant of David, according to my gospel, for which I suffer hardship even to imprisonment as a criminal; but the word of God is not imprisoned. For this reason I endure all things for the sake of those who are chosen, so that they also may obtain the salvation which is in Christ Jesus and with it eternal glory.

—2 Timothy 2:8–10

Where is Paul and why is he there? Why is he enduring all things?

When Paul says he will endure all things, he is not kidding. In 2 Corinthians 11, we learn that he was not only imprisoned, he was also beaten numerous times (with a whip five times and with a rod three times) and stoned once. He was in constant danger from rivers, robbers, Gentiles and Jews, false brethren, the wilderness, and the seas. (He was stranded on the open seas and shipwrecked at least three times.) He had many sleepless nights, often went without food, in the cold, without clothing, not to mention the daily pressure of his concern for the churches.

Potential Perfected

Any one of these situations could have been a life-bondage issue. But this is the Paul who talks about being more than a conqueror, of a momentary light affliction that produces an eternal weight of glory. When you can grasp this "momentary light affliction" idea and really get it in our spirit, you know it is God working, and you can see it from an eternal perspective.

Paul does not ignore his troubles. He admits to being afflicted, but not crushed; perplexed, but not despairing; persecuted but not forsaken; struck down, but not destroyed; always carrying about the dying of the Lord Jesus within him so that the life of Jesus could be manifested to others (2 Corinthians 4:8–10).

Read 2 Corinthians 4:11–12 and catch his attitude.

> For we who live are constantly being delivered over to death for Jesus' sake, so that the life of Jesus also may be manifested in our mortal flesh. So death works in us, but life in you.
> —2 Corinthians 4:11–12

Example #4 - From Peter to the scattered aliens

> But you are a chosen race, a royal priesthood, a holy nation, a people for God's own possession, so that you may proclaim the excellencies of Him who has called you out of darkness into His marvelous light; for you once were not a people, but now you are the people of God; you had not received mercy, but now you have received mercy. Beloved, I urge you as aliens and strangers to abstain from fleshly lusts which wage war against the soul. Keep your behavior excellent among the Gentiles, so that in the thing in which they slander you as evildoers, they may because of your good deeds, as they observe them, glorify God in the day of visitation.
> —1 Peter 2:9–12

What are the people to do? Why are they told to do this?

Example #5 - Peter to those who have the same kind of faith

> But false prophets also arose among the people, just as there will also be false teachers among you, who will secretly introduce destructive heresies, even denying the Master who bought them, bringing swift destruction upon themselves. Many will follow their sensuality, and because of them the way of the truth will be maligned.
> —2 Peter 2:1–2

False prophets and teachers arose among the people. Who will follow them, even though they deny the Master? What has happened to truth?

You therefore, beloved, knowing this beforehand, be on your guard so that you are not carried away by the error of unprincipled men and fall from your own steadfastness, but grow in the grace and knowledge of our Lord and Savior Jesus Christ. To Him be the glory, both now and to the day of eternity. Amen.

—2 Peter 3:17–18

What is Peter's instruction to the people? How can they remain steadfast? In what are they to grow?

Example #6 - From Jesus to the Father

"Sanctify them in the truth; Your word is truth. As You sent Me into the world, I also have sent them into the world. For their sakes I sanctify Myself, that they themselves also may be sanctified in truth. I do not ask on behalf of these alone, but for those also who believe in Me through their word; that they may all be one; even as You, Father, are in Me and I in You, that they also may be in Us, so that the world may believe that You sent Me. The glory which You have given Me I have given to them, that they may be one, just as We are one; I in them and You in Me, that they may be perfected in unity, so that the world may know that You sent Me, and loved them, even as You have loved Me. Father, I desire that they also, whom You have given Me, be with Me where I am, so that they may see My glory which You have given Me, for You loved Me before the foundation of the world."

—John 17:17–24

Potential Perfected 175

Where has Jesus sent His disciples? What is His request on behalf of all believers? Why does Jesus give the believers the glory that the Father gave Him? What does He want the world to know? In what are they are to be perfected? Can you tell why?

Summarize the reasons for bondage that you found by studying the following Scriptures:

Example #1 – From the Sermon on the Mount

Example #2 - From John recording how Jesus healed a blind man

Example #3 - From Paul to Timothy

Example #4 - From Peter to the scattered aliens

Example #5 – From Peter to those who had the same kind of faith

Example #6 - From Jesus to the Father

What is the common ground in these six examples?

    We have found that God allows bondage for a number of reasons, and I am sure there are many more. We saw Joseph in bondage, but understood his purpose was to go before Israel to preserve a nation. (God had a covenant to keep and an eternal purpose to fulfill.) We saw Israel in bondage so that the Egyptians, Pharaoh, and even the Israelites would know who God was. We saw Israel in bondage because they were rebellious, refused to listen to God, had things all turned around, and had forgotten who was in charge. We saw the bondage and affliction of Job so that he would not only hear God, but see Him as well. We also saw Job's bondage used to get his friends on the right track. We saw David's bondage as a result of willful sin. The result of his release from bondage was to desire to praise God and instruct other transgressors about God. We also saw that David understood his purpose, that he was made king, and that God exalted his kingdom for the sake of the people.
    In the New Testament, we saw those who were persecuted called "blessed." They were to be light and salt in the world so that God would be glorified. We saw a man born blind so that God's works could be glorified in him. We saw Paul in 2 Timothy enduring all things for the sake of the chosen so they could obtain salvation. We saw Peter admonishing the aliens to show forth the praises of God and to have excellent behavior so that those who saw them could glorify God in the day of visitation. Peter instructs the believers to be on guard since there are false prophets and teachers among them. They are to grow in the knowledge and grace of Jesus Christ. Finally, we saw Jesus praying that believers all over the world would be one, that they

Potential Perfected

would be perfected in unity so the world would believe that He was sent by the Father, so the world would believe in Jesus.

Those in bondage always have a way out. Some bondage situations could have been avoided by consistently trusting God, knowing His Word, and applying it. Self-inflicted bondage, willful sin, rebellion, lack of trust, etc. are situations in which we do not want to find ourselves. We should not make plans to go there, and if we are already there, we need to get out!

> For what credit is there if, when you sin and are harshly treated, you endure it with patience? But if when you do what is right and suffer for it you patiently endure it, this finds favor with God.
>
> —1 Peter 2:20

Those in bondage always have an impact on others, whether to discipline, to point in the right direction, to correct, or to prepare for the next assignment. Hold on to your integrity, grow in the knowledge of Jesus Christ, and walk and live like you belong to God. God wants everyone to know that He is God and that He alone is to be glorified.

> "I am the Lord, and there is no other; besides Me there is no God. I will gird you, though you have not known Me; that men may know from the rising to the setting of the sun That there is no one besides Me. I am the Lord, and there is no other.
>
> —Isaiah 45:5–6

How would God have you respond to today's lesson?

Living in the Freedom of Christ

Chapter Twenty-Six
___

You'd Better Know It!

If Christ has set you free, you are free indeed. So, how can you consistently live in the freedom that is available to all believers? How do you avoid the bondages, the captivity, and the traps that are set for you?

For the truth to make us free, we must know it, pray it, and obey it. The Word will perform its work in you if you believe. (See 1 Thessalonians 2:13.)

Read the following passages and record the principles that will help you live free.

I will walk at liberty, for I seek Your precepts. I will also speak of Your testimonies before kings and shall not be ashamed. I shall delight in Your commandments, Which I love. And I shall lift up my hands to Your commandments, Which I love; And I will meditate on Your statutes.
—Psalm 119:45–48

WORD STUDY

The Hebrew word for "liberty" in this verse is *rachab*, meaning "in any (or every) direction, literally or figuratively; broad, large, at liberty, proud, wide." His precepts, testimonies, commandments, and statutes all generally refer to God's law, His precepts, His Word.

The psalmist says in verse 45 that he will walk at liberty. While he is walking at liberty, what else does he say he will do in that passage? Where is his major emphasis? Record your findings below.

O Lord, surely I am Your servant, I am Your servant, the son of Your handmaid, You have loosed my bonds. To You I shall offer a sacrifice of thanksgiving, And call upon the name of the Lord.

—Psalm 116:16–17

What has God done? What will the servant do?

Read on to find out what we need to know.

For this reason I too, having heard of the faith in the Lord Jesus which exists among you and your love for all the saints, do not cease giving thanks for you, while making mention of you in

You'd Better Know It!

my prayers; that the God of our Lord Jesus Christ, the Father of glory, may give to you a spirit of wisdom and of revelation in the knowledge of Him.

—Ephesians 1:15–17

Paul is writing to the church at Ephesus. He lived there for about three years, reasoning with and persuading both Jews and Gentiles about the Kingdom of God. He is now writing as a prisoner from Rome. He has just told them they have been blessed with all spiritual blessings. In the verses above, what has he heard about them and what is he praying that God will give them?

WORD STUDY

The Greek word for "knowledge" here is *epignosis*, meaning "recognition; i.e. (by implication), full discernment, acknowledgement." It expresses a more thorough participation in the acquiring of knowledge on the part of the learner. In the New Testament, it often refers to knowledge, which very powerfully influences the form of religious life, a knowledge laying claim to personal involvement.

Based on this definition, Paul wants them to recognize and participate in what they know about God.

I pray that the eyes of your heart may be enlightened, so that you will know what is the hope of His calling, what are the riches of the glory of His inheritance in the saints, and what is the surpassing greatness of His power toward us who believe. These are in accordance with the working of the strength of His might which He brought about in Christ, when He raised Him from the dead and seated Him at His right hand in the heavenly places, far above all rule and authority and power and dominion, and every name that is named, not only in this age but also in the one to come.

—Ephesians 1:18–21

What three things does Paul want them to know? What has to happen to the eyes of their hearts?

WORD STUDY

"Hope" in the Greek is *elpis,* from a primary *elpo* ("to anticipate, usually with pleasure"). It refers to "expectation (abstractly or concretely) or confidence: faith, hope, desire of some good with expectation of obtaining it." It is used especially to refer to those who experience the hope of salvation through Christ, eternal life.

Paul wants them to be absolutely certain about and have confidence in their salvation (His calling), to be aware of the glory of their inheritance (His inheritance), and to know about the surpassing greatness of the power (His power) for all believers. He talked about their calling in Ephesians 1:1–14, and he talks about the power from above in Ephesians 1: 19–22.

> ...and what is the surpassing greatness of His power toward us who believe. These are in accordance with the working of the strength of His might which He brought about in Christ, when He raised Him from the dead and seated Him at His right hand in the heavenly places, far above all rule and authority and power and dominion, and every name that is named, not only in this age but also in the one to come. And He put all things in subjection under His feet, and gave Him as head over all things to the church, which is His body, the fullness of Him who fills all in all.
>
> —Ephesians 1:19–22

WORD STUDY

The Greek word for "power" in verse 19 is *dunamis,* meaning "force (literally or figuratively); specifically, miraculous power (usually by implication, a miracle itself):– ability, abundance, meaning, might(-ily, -y, -y deed), (worker of) miracle(-s), power, strength, violence, mighty (wonderful) work."

The third thing Paul wants them to know is the magnitude of God's abundant, miracle working power. What is all this in accordance with? To whom is it available?

This is the same power that God brought about in Christ. Record what God did and what Jesus is above.

The same power that raised Jesus from the dead and seated Him on the right hand of God the Father is available to all who believe. As we believe we are free and live that way, God continues to work His mighty power in us.

> So then, my beloved, just as you have always obeyed, not as in my presence only, but now much more in my absence, work out your salvation with fear and trembling; for it is God who is at work in you, both to will and to work for His good pleasure.
> —Philippians 2:12–13

Whose salvation are you working out? How? Who is working in you to get it done?

WORD STUDY

The Greek for "work out" is *katergazomai*, meaning "to work fully; i.e., accomplish; by implication, to finish, fashion:–cause, to (deed), perform, work (out)."
The Greek word for "work" (used twice) is *energeo*, meaning "to be active, efficient:–do, (be) effectual (fervent), be mighty in, shew forth self, work (effectually in)."
The Greek word for "pleasure" is *eudokia*, meaning "satisfaction; i.e. (subjectively), delight, or (objectively) kindness, wish, purpose:–desire, good pleasure (will)."
All these words are in the present tense in Greek, which means continuous action.

The issue here is not getting saved, but living in the freedom that we have as believers. We are commanded to "work out our own salvation" (living holy because we are saved). We are accomplishing what God intends for our life. God is continuously working His will (His purpose) in us as well as working His work in us. He is doing it for His good pleasure, His delight, and His satisfaction in His kindness and for His purpose.

If God is working in the believer to will and do of His good pleasure, is there any reason we cannot live in the freedom that He provides? If you can think of a reason, write it down.

Chapter Twenty-Seven
___

PLEASING HIM

Living in the freedom Christ provides means being totally dependent on God and striving to please Him in every respect. You may not win a lot of friends that way. For sure, somebody is going to be unhappy. You may not influence some folks, but if you stay on course, you will please God.

Read the following Scriptures and recognize your purpose.

> For this reason also, since the day we heard of it, we have not ceased to pray for you and to ask that you may be filled with the knowledge of His will in all spiritual wisdom and understanding, so that you will walk in a manner worthy of the Lord, to please Him in all respects, bearing fruit in every good work and increasing in the knowledge of God.
> —Colossians 1:9–10

Paul is writing to the church at Colossae from prison in Rome. He has heard about their faith in Jesus and their love for all the saints. (Note: The word for "knowledge" is the same as we discussed in the previous chapter, meaning to recognize and participate in what they know about God.) What is his prayer for them? Why?

How are they to walk?

Who are they to please?

What kind of work will be the result?

In what are they to increase?

…strengthened with all power, according to His glorious might, for the attaining of all steadfastness and patience; joyously giving thanks to the Father, who has qualified us to share in the inheritance of the saints in Light. For He rescued us from the domain of darkness, and transferred us to the kingdom of His beloved Son, in whom we have redemption, the forgiveness of sins.

—Colossians 1:11–14

Pleasing Him

Where will they get the power and might?

What will they attain?

For what has God qualified them?

What has God rescued them from and to where have they been transferred?

WORD STUDY

The Greek word for "transferred" is *methistemi,* meaning "to transfer; i.e., carry away, depose or (figuratively) exchange, seduce:–put out, remove, translate, turn away."

After being rescued and transferred what is the final result?

How can we please Him? Take Him at His word. Our responsibility is to walk in a manner worthy of the call. That means our walk should be equal to His call. He provides the strength as we increase in the knowledge of Him. As He strengthens us with all might, we are able to bear fruit and attain steadfastness and patience.

Can you also see *why* we are to please Him? He is the one who qualified us for an inheritance, rescued and delivered us from darkness, transferred us into His kingdom, redeemed us, and forgave us of our sins. Is there any reason we cannot live in the freedom He provides? If you can think of a reason, write it down.

In order to please God, your actions may have to change and your friends may change as well.

> Now flee from youthful lusts and pursue righteousness, faith, love and peace, with those who call on the Lord from a pure heart.
>
> —2 Timothy 2:22

From what will you flee? What will you pursue?

With whom will you run?

Of course you cannot listen to those who are not pursuing righteousness. However, even well-meaning saints who call on the Lord with a pure heart may give you conflicting instructions. You have to stand firm on what the Lord has told you personally.

In Acts 20, Paul met with the elders from Ephesus and told them where he was going.

> And now, behold, bound in spirit, I am on my way to Jerusalem, not knowing what will happen to me there, except that the Holy Spirit solemnly testifies to me in every city, saying that

bonds and afflictions await me. But I do not consider my life of any account as dear to myself, so that I may finish my course and the ministry which I received from the Lord Jesus, to testify solemnly of the gospel of the grace of God.

—Acts 20:22–24

Where is he going?

What has the Holy Spirit told him?

What is his attitude?

What is his assignment and who gave it to him?

In Acts 21, Paul was on his way to Jerusalem and he stopped in Caesarea at Philip's house. While he was there, a prophet named Agabus also stopped by. Read the following verses and note the interchange.

As we were staying there for some days, a prophet named Agabus came down from Judea. And coming to us, he took Paul's belt and bound his own feet and hands, and said, "This is what the Holy Spirit says: 'In this way the Jews at Jerusalem will bind the man who owns this belt and deliver him into the hands of the Gentiles.'" When we had heard this, we as well as the local residents began begging him not to go up to Jerusalem. Then Paul answered, "What are you doing, weeping and breaking my heart? For I am ready not only to be bound, but even to die at Jerusalem for the name of the Lord Jesus." And since he would not be persuaded, we fell silent, remarking, "The will of the Lord be done!"

—Acts 21:10–14

What is the problem?

Is this new information for Paul?

What is his attitude? Why? What was the assignment and who gave it to him?

What was their response?

What does God require to please Him? Going to Jerusalem? Witnessing and bringing one soul to Christ for every year He allows you to live? Singing in a choir, ushering, showing up at church every Sunday, doing your daily devotions? Teaching? Preaching? What?

And without faith it is impossible to please Him, for he who comes to God must believe that He is and that He is a rewarder of those who seek Him.

—Hebrews 11:6

Pleasing Him

From this verse, what will please God?

What specifically must you believe?

What will He do for those who seek Him?

WORD STUDY

The Greek word for "seek" is *ekzeteo*, meaning "to search out; i.e. (figuratively), investigate, crave, demand, worship; seek after (carefully, diligently); to seek diligently or earnestly after (namely God) with a sincere and earnest desire to obtain His favor."

There is no pleasing God if you do not believe. Just believe that He exists, that He is real, and that He will reward or do good to those who worship and investigate Him, crave and seek after Him with a sincere and earnest desire to obtain His favor.

If we know the promises of God, not just that He can, but that He will, we can move on His Word. If the only way we can please God is by faith, and He is constantly testing our faith, shouldn't we diligently seek Him?

Do you truly believe that He will reward those who go after Him? Are you receiving all the blessings God has for you? Are you missing any?

What is the basis of such strong belief? Simply believing God and His faithfulness.

God is faithful to keep His covenant, His agreement.
God's faithfulness surrounds us. He is perfect, and He will never fail you.

God is not man and He will not lie; if He said it, He will do it.

God will not allow you to be in a situation you can't handle, but He will provide a way of escape so you can bear it

God will complete the work begun in you.

God has strengthened you and will protect you.

God has forgiven those who believe Him from the power, penalty, and guilt of sin.

God is always a refuge and strength and will hide you in His shelter if you abide in Him.

God will keep you in perfect peace if you focus on Him.

God has always done and will continue to do everything He has said He will do.

God never changes, so His faithfulness is forever.

You can believe Him because He is faithful.

When you believe God, you will be like a tree planted by the rivers of water.

When you believe God, you will not fear.

When you believe God, His grace will be sufficient.

When you believe God, your prayers are full of thankfulness and not a rehearsal of woes.

When you believe God, though you may be in trouble, your heart is not troubled.

When you believe God, life is not like Russian roulette; His promises are sure!

Just as Noah built an ark when God said to build—you build.

Just as Abraham believed God could call into being things that did not exist— you believe God.

Just as Joseph believed God in the pit and the prison and was elevated to the palace—you believe God.

Just as Deborah moved into battle with Barak when God said, "This is the day"—you move.

Just as Jehoshaphat did not know what to do, but kept his eyes on God—let God fight your battles.

Just as Paul believed He would finish His course with joy—finish your course.

Just as Job believed that although God was slaying him, he could still trust Him—you trust him.

Just as Joshua believed that the wall would fall—you begin to march around the obstacles.

Just as Caleb believed they were well able to overcome—live like you are overcoming.

Pleasing Him

Just as three teenage boys believed God could deliver them in the fire—you expect deliverance.

Just as Moses endured as seeing Him who is unseen—you endure, believing God.

Believing God, trusting Him leaves no doubts, but brings hope, peace, confidence, and increased faith. Believe God in the good times, the bad times, and the ugly times, for He is faithful. If you want to please Him, you must trust Him, whether you see the solution or not.

Is it so difficult to believe that God exists and that He wants to do good to those who believe in Him? Is there any reason we cannot live in the freedom He provides? If you can think of a reason, write it down.

Chapter Twenty-Eight
_____

KEEP IT CLEAN

Living in the freedom God provides means you keep your life clean. When you sin, confess it. When you confess, repent. Don't get caught in a sin trap and stay there. While Satan is the accuser of the brethren, we have a Mediator and an Advocate who ever lives to make intercession. You know His name. It's Jesus!

Sin is always a bad choice. Look at how God responds when we don't respond to Him as we should.

> How long, O naive ones, will you love being simple-minded? And scoffers delight themselves in scoffing And fools hate knowledge? Turn to my reproof, Behold, I will pour out my spirit on you; I will make my words known to you. Because I called and you refused, I stretched out my hand and no one paid attention; and you neglected all my counsel And did not want my reproof.
>
> —Proverbs 1:22–25

What is the description of those in this passage? What do they hate?

Note: Both *naïve* and *simple-minded* have the same meaning as *foolish*.

What does God offer in verse 23?

What is their response?

I will also laugh at your calamity; I will mock when your dread comes, when your dread comes like a storm And your calamity comes like a whirlwind, When distress and anguish come upon you. Then they will call on me, but I will not answer; They will seek me diligently but they will not find me, because they hated knowledge And did not choose the fear of the Lord. They would not accept my counsel, they spurned all my reproof.
—Proverbs 1:26–30

What is God's response? Why?

Look at the passage again. Does this contradict Hebrews 11:6, which says He will reward those who diligently seek Him? Why or why not?

Why won't God answer them? Why is He allowing them to stay in the storm (dread) and in the whirlwind (calamity)?

Can we pray, "O Father, please bless us, but don't change us?" Can we ask God to deliver us from a problem, or to work in our lives in whatever way He wishes, and then disregard Him? Isn't this the deception that many are living under today?

So they shall eat of the fruit of their own way And be satiated with their own devices. For the waywardness of the naive will kill them, And the complacency of fools will destroy them. But he who listens to me shall live securely And will be at ease from the dread of evil.
—Proverbs 1:31–33

What does God promise to those who live foolishly?

What does God promise to those who will listen?

God provided freedom, but it is on His terms and none other. You have to work pretty hard to stay in captivity. Neglect God's counsel; refuse His hand and His reproof (correction); do not listen to Him, and do not fear Him.

According to Proverbs 1:31–33, what will waywardness (turning away from God) do?

Is there any reason we cannot live in the freedom He provides? If you can think of a reason, write it down.

Read Psalm 107 for a different response.

There were those who dwelt in darkness and in the shadow of death, Prisoners in misery and chains, because they had rebelled against the words of God And spurned the counsel of the Most High. Therefore He humbled their heart with labor; They stumbled and there was none to help. Then they cried out to the Lord in their trouble; He saved them out of their distresses. He brought them out of darkness and the shadow of death And broke their bands apart.
—Psalm 107:10–14

How are the people described? Where are they?

Keep It Clean

Why are they there? Sound familiar?

What did God do? Who helped them?

How do they get out of trouble?

Let them give thanks to the Lord for His lovingkindness, And for His wonders to the sons of men! For He has shattered gates of bronze And cut bars of iron asunder. Fools, because of their rebellious way, And because of their iniquities, were afflicted. Their soul abhorred all kinds of food, And they drew near to the gates of death. Then they cried out to the Lord in their trouble; He saved them out of their distresses. He sent His word and healed them, And delivered them from their destructions. Let them give thanks to the Lord for His lovingkindness, And for His wonders to the sons of men! Let them also offer sacrifices of thanksgiving, And tell of His works with joyful singing.

—Psalm 107:15–22

Why should they be grateful? Why were they in trouble?

How far did they let sin go before they cried to the Lord? Did it affect their bodies? Did it affect their souls? How?

How were they healed?

Why should they be grateful? What else could they do?

Read Psalm 32 and see what happens with unconfessed sin.

> When I kept silent about my sin, my body wasted away Through my groaning all day long. For day and night Your hand was heavy upon me; my vitality was drained away as with the fever heat of summer. Selah.
>
> —Psalm 32:3–4

Record what happened to the psalmist's body when he kept silent about his sin.

He would not confess his sin, but what did he do all day long?

Keep It Clean

Whose hand is heavy on him? What else is happening to him because of this unconfessed sin?

> I acknowledged my sin to You, and my iniquity I did not hide; I said, "I will confess my transgressions to the Lord"; and You forgave the guilt of my sin. Selah. Therefore, let everyone who is godly pray to You in a time when You may be found; Surely in a flood of great waters they will not reach him. You are my hiding place; You preserve me from trouble; You surround me with songs of deliverance. Selah.
>
> —Psalm 32:5–7

Once the sin is acknowledged, what does God do?

Was it the sin or the guilt of the sin that was the problem here?

After forgiveness, what is the psalmist's recommendation to others?

What does the Psalmist say about God?

Is there any reason we cannot live in the freedom He provides? If you can think of a reason, write it down.

What shall we do with this freedom we have? For one thing, don't abuse it. Read the following verses and record your observations.

> But take care that this liberty of yours does not somehow become a stumbling block to the weak.
> —1 Corinthians 8:9

> It was for freedom that Christ set us free; therefore keep standing firm and do not be subject again to a yoke of slavery.
> —Galatians 5:1

> For you were called to freedom, brethren; only do not turn your freedom into an opportunity for the flesh, but through love serve one another.
> —Galatians 5:13

> But I say, walk by the Spirit, and you will not carry out the desire of the flesh.
> —Galatians 5:16

> For such is the will of God that by doing right you may silence the ignorance of foolish men. Act as free men, and do not use your freedom as a covering for evil, but use it as bondslaves of God.
> —1 Peter 2:15–16

Keep It Clean

Summarize all that you have learned about living in God's freedom. What is the plan that God has for your life? Is there any reason you cannot live in the freedom He provides? If you can think of a reason, write it down.

Depending on the Guidance of the Spirit

Chapter Twenty-Nine

SPIRITUAL MIND-SET

God has also provided help for us in the person of the Holy Spirit. As you look at the following passages, consider His work in your life. Look for the clear distinction between the mind-sets of those who are His and those who are not.

Read and record your findings, marking *Spirit* as you read.

Romans 8:3–4 For what the Law could not do, weak as it was through the flesh, God did: sending His own Son in the likeness of sinful flesh and as an offering for sin, He condemned sin in the flesh, so that the requirement of the Law might be fulfilled in us, who do not walk according to the flesh but according to the Spirit.

What did God do?

What did His Son do?

What was the result for us? How are we to walk?

> For those who are according to the flesh set their minds on the things of the flesh, but those who are according to the Spirit, the things of the Spirit. For the mind set on the flesh is death, but the mind set on the Spirit is life and peace, because the mind set on the flesh is hostile toward God; for it does not subject itself to the law of God, for it is not even able to do so, and those who are in the flesh cannot please God. However, you are not in the flesh but in the Spirit, if indeed the Spirit of God dwells in you. But if anyone does not have the Spirit of Christ, he does not belong to Him.
>
> —Romans 8:5–8

Make a list of what you see about the Holy Spirit and about the flesh:

Holy Spirit   **Flesh**

According to this passage, is there a way we can always have peace? How?

List two reasons the mind set on the flesh cannot subject itself to the law of God.

Spiritual Mind-set

How can you know if you are in the Spirit?

How is someone who does not have the Spirit of Christ described?

According to the passage above, can a person belong to Him (be saved) and not have the Holy Spirit?

If Christ is in you, though the body is dead because of sin, yet the spirit is alive because of righteousness. But if the Spirit of Him who raised Jesus from the dead dwells in you, He who raised Christ Jesus from the dead will also give life to your mortal bodies through His Spirit who dwells in you. So then, brethren, we are under obligation, not to the flesh, to live according to the flesh–for if you are living according to the flesh, you must die; but if by the Spirit you are putting to death the deeds of the body, you will live.

—Romans 8:10–13

Continue your list on Spirit and flesh:

Spirit   **Flesh**

What happens to those who are living under the influence of the Spirit?

What is to be the believer's relationship to the flesh?

What will happen if we do not respond when the flesh makes a demand or a request? What is your mind-set about the flesh?

For all who are being led by the Spirit of God, these are sons of God. For you have not received a spirit of slavery leading to fear again, but you have received a spirit of adoption as sons by which we cry out, "Abba! Father!" The Spirit Himself testifies with our spirit that we are children of God, and if children, heirs also, heirs of God and fellow heirs with Christ, if indeed we suffer with Him so that we may also be glorified with Him.

—Romans 8:14–17

How are the sons of God described?

What does the Spirit of God do in the lives of the children of God?

What happens to those who suffer with Him? What is your mind-set about suffering?

Spiritual Mind-set

Is there any reason you cannot live in the freedom Christ provides? Is there any reason you cannot depend on the influence of the Holy Spirit in your life? If you can think of a reason, write it down.

Chapter Thirty

WHY GOD PROMISED HIS SPIRIT

Israel is in rebellion. They have been disobedient to God. But God has a plan! Read the following verses, marking *Lord* and any related pronouns (*Me, My,* etc.).

Then the word of the Lord came to me saying, "Son of man, when the house of Israel was living in their own land, they defiled it by their ways and their deeds; their way before Me was like the uncleanness of a woman in her impurity. Therefore I poured out My wrath on them for the blood which they had shed on the land, because they had defiled it with their idols. Also I scattered them among the nations and they were dispersed throughout the lands. According to their ways and their deeds I judged them. When they came to the nations where they went, they profaned My holy name, because it was said of them, 'These are the people of the Lord; yet they have come out of His land.'"

—Ezekiel 36:16–20

Why is God so angry with Israel? Specifically, what did Israel do?

Read on, continuing to mark any reference to God.

"But I had concern for My holy name, which the house of Israel had profaned among the nations where they went. Therefore say to the house of Israel, 'Thus says the Lord GOD, "It is not for your sake, O house of Israel, that I am about to act, but for My holy name, which you have profaned among the nations where you went. I will vindicate the holiness of My great name which has been profaned among the nations, which you have profaned in their midst. Then the nations will know that I am the Lord," declares the Lord GOD, "when I prove Myself holy among you in their sight."'"

—Ezekiel 36

What did Israel do?

Where did they do it?

How did this affect God? What was His concern?

How is God going to vindicate the holiness of His great name? How will the nations know that He is God?

Why God Promised His Spirit

"For I will take you from the nations, gather you from all the lands and bring you into your own land. Then I will sprinkle clean water on you, and you will be clean; I will cleanse you from all your filthiness and from all your idols. Moreover, I will give you a new heart and put a new spirit within you; and I will remove the heart of stone from your flesh and give you a heart of flesh. I will put My Spirit within you and cause you to walk in My statutes, and you will be careful to observe My ordinances. You will live in the land that I gave to your forefathers; so you will be My people, and I will be your God."

—Ezekiel 36:24–28

God has said He would prove Himself holy among the Israelites in the sight of the other nations. What was He going to do to Israel to make Himself known to the nations?

What would they receive that was new? What was He going to remove?

Where was He going to put His Spirit? What would be the result?

Remember how this started? God was angry with Israel because they were profaning His name among the nations, by their ways and deeds, by worshipping idols, and by their overall lifestyles. They were ruining His reputation and He had concern for His name. So in order that the nations would know that He was and is God, He intended to clean Israel up, to give them a new heart and a new spirit. His plan was to put His Spirit within them and cause them to walk in His statutes and His commandments so that the nations would know that He was and is God. And He did! He does the same for us.

Read on as Jesus speaks to His disciples.

"If you love Me, you will keep My commandments. I will ask the Father, and He will give you another Helper, that He may be with you forever; that is the Spirit of truth, whom the world cannot receive, because it does not see Him or know Him, but you know Him because He abides with you and will be in you."

—John 14:15–17

Who is Jesus going to send?

Why can't the world receive the Spirit?

Where will He live?

"But the Helper, the Holy Spirit, whom the Father will send in My name, He will teach you all things, and bring to your remembrance all that I said to you. Peace I leave with you; My peace I give to you; not as the world gives do I give to you. Do not let your heart be troubled, nor let it be fearful."

—John 14:26–27

Who is being sent?

Why God Promised His Spirit

Who is sending Him and in whose name?

What help will He provide?

What is the promise and instruction?

"But I tell you the truth, it is to your advantage that I go away; for if I do not go away, the Helper will not come to you; but if I go, I will send Him to you. And He, when He comes, will convict the world concerning sin and righteousness and judgment; concerning sin, because they do not believe in Me; and concerning righteousness, because I go to the Father and you no longer see Me; and concerning judgment, because the ruler of this world has been judged."
—John 16:7–11

List the responsibilities of the Holy Spirit.

Where will He live?

How will the world be convicted?

If the world is not being convicted, does it have anything to do with how believers live?

Can you see why God has given us His Spirit? His indwelling is not for us only, not just so we can feel good, not only for our praise, not just for pew-warming and activities inside our church buildings, but also so that the world can see who God is in us. Can you see why God wants us to live in the freedom of Christ and under the influence of the Holy Spirit? Why?

"I have many more things to say to you, but you cannot bear them now. But when He, the Spirit of truth, comes, He will guide you into all the truth; for He will not speak on His own initiative, but whatever He hears, He will speak; and He will disclose to you what is to come. He will glorify Me, for He will take of Mine and will disclose it to you. All things that the Father has are Mine; therefore I said that He takes of Mine and will disclose it to you."

—John 16:12–15

List the responsibilities of the Holy Spirit.

Why God Promised His Spirit

WORD STUDY

The Greek word for "disclose" is *anaggello,* meaning "to announce (in detail); declare, rehearse, report, show, speak, tell."

What is the Holy Spirit going to announce, to show, to tell? Whom will He tell?

Whom will He glorify?

In Acts 1, just prior to Jesus' ascension, He tells His disciples again that the Holy Spirit would be coming soon, as promised by the Father and as we read in Ezekiel 36. He told them that when the Spirit came upon them they would receive power and they would be witnesses. In Acts 2, on the Day of Pentecost, the promised Holy Spirit comes and we see the beginning of the church.

Read the following passage and record what you see about the Holy Spirit.

> Or do you not know that your body is a temple of the Holy Spirit who is in you, whom you have from God, and that you are not your own? For you have been bought with a price: therefore glorify God in your body.
> —1 Corinthians 6:19–20

Where does the Spirit live?

To whom do you belong?

What is the responsibility of the believer? Who will work through you to get His work done? Who else?

Summarize all that you have learned about the Holy Spirit's work in your life.

What is the Spirit of God saying to you about all you have studied today? Is there any reason you cannot live in the freedom that Christ provides? Is there any reason you cannot depend on the influence of the Spirit in your life? If you can think of a reason, write it down.

Chapter Thirty-One

INTERCEDING IN THE DEEP

When Paul wrote to the church in Corinth, they were involved in numerous problems, most of them concerning how to interact with one another and with the world. There were quarrels and divisions within the church and problems outside the church that influenced those within. Corinth, the chief city of Greece, was overrun with philosophers, orators, Greek gods, temple prostitutes, and gross immorality. Paul wrote to address problems the Christians were experiencing and to answer their questions.

In Chapter 2 he makes sure they know that he did not come with superior speech or wisdom and that his main purpose was Jesus Christ and Him crucified. Read the following passage and record what you see about his message and the Holy Spirit. Mark *Spirit* as you read.

> I was with you in weakness and in fear and in much trembling, and my message and my preaching were not in persuasive words of wisdom, but in demonstration of the Spirit and of power, so that your faith would not rest on the wisdom of men, but on the power of God.
> —1 Corinthians 2:3–5

Why was Paul concerned about the manner in which his message was delivered? What did he want to be the basis of their faith?

Read on, marking *things*.

> But just as it is written, "Things which eye has not seen and ear has not heard, and which have not entered the heart of man, all that God has prepared for those who love Him."
> —1 Corinthians 2:9

In this verse, Paul is quoting Isaiah. What "things" has God prepared?

For whom are they prepared?

Read on, continuing to mark *Spirit* and *things* as you read.

> For to us God revealed them through the Spirit; for the Spirit searches all things, even the depths of God. For who among men knows the thoughts of a man except the spirit of the man which is in him? Even so the thoughts of God no one knows except the Spirit of God.
> —1 Corinthians 2:10–11

How are the "things" revealed? (You may have to go back to verse 9.)

Interceding in the Deep

What does the Spirit do?

Who knows God's thoughts?

Who is revealing these "things" to us?

Read on, continuing to mark *Spirit* and *things*.

> Now we have received, not the spirit of the world, but the Spirit who is from God, so that we may know the things freely given to us by God, which things we also speak, not in words taught by human wisdom, but in those taught by the Spirit, combining spiritual thoughts with spiritual words.
> —1 Corinthians 2:12–13

Whose Spirit do believers have? Why?

What do you see about the "things?"

What is being contrasted?

What two things are being combined?

Whose thoughts and whose words?

To whom are they revealed? By whom?

Read on, continuing to mark *Spirit* and *things*.

But a natural man does not accept the things of the Spirit of God, for they are foolishness to him; and he cannot understand them, because they are spiritually appraised. But he who is spiritual appraises all things, yet he himself is appraised by no one. For who has known the mind of the Lord, that he will instruct Him? But we have the mind of Christ.

—1 Corinthians 2:14–16

What do you see about the Spirit?

Interceding in the Deep

What do you see about the "things?"

Who has the mind of Christ? Why?

Read the following passage, marking *Spirit* and *things*. Also mark *know* or *knows*.

In the same way the Spirit also helps our weakness; for we do not know how to pray as we should, but the Spirit Himself intercedes for us with groanings too deep for words; and He who searches the hearts knows what the mind of the Spirit is, because He intercedes for the saints according to the will of God. And we know that God causes all things to work together for good to those who love God, to those who are called according to His purpose.
—Romans 8:26–28

What do we see as the responsibility of the Spirit in these verses?

Why do we need help?

The Spirit will intercede in our prayers, making sure they line up with the will of God. Could that be why we sometimes get answers so unlike what we pray for? We look for one answer and God sends another answer, one that lines up with His will. What is the end result?

Summarize the help that the Holy Spirit provides for believers.

I know He is speaking to your heart today. Write out your response as a prayer to God.

Is there any reason you cannot live in the freedom that Christ provides? Is there any reason you cannot depend on the influence of the Spirit in your life? If you can think of a reason, write it down.

Now the Lord is the Spirit, and where the Spirit of the Lord is, there is liberty.
—2 Corinthians 3:17

Relying on the Word of God

Chapter Thirty-Two

LET THE WORD DWELL RICHLY

When Paul wrote to the Colossians, he was in prison in Rome. This group of believers, although known for their faith and love, were being influenced by philosophy and empty deception, according to the traditions of men and the world rather than according to Christ. He tells them to devote themselves to prayer. He also instructs them in how to handle the Word.

> Let the word of Christ richly dwell within you, with all wisdom teaching and admonishing one another with psalms and hymns and spiritual songs, singing with thankfulness in your hearts to God.
>
> —Colossians 3:16

WORD STUDY

The Greek word for "richly" is *plousios,* meaning "copiously, abundantly, richly."

What are we to do with the Word?

Notice Paul's emphasis on their personal relationship with Christ and His Word. Based on the definition of the word 'richly', how much of the word of Christ is too much?

How is the teaching to be done?

Did you notice Paul does not say, "with all knowledge" or "with all intelligence" or "with all charisma"? How are they to 'let the word of Christ dwell' and whom are they to admonish?

In this next passage, Paul gives some final instructions and says good-bye to the saints he has spent about three years with.

> From Miletus he sent to Ephesus and called to him the elders of the church. And when they had come to him, he said to them, "You yourselves know, from the first day that I set foot in Asia, how I was with you the whole time, serving the Lord with all humility and with tears and with trials which came upon me through the plots of the Jews; how I did not shrink from declaring to you anything that was profitable, and teaching you publicly and from house to house, solemnly testifying to both Jews and Greeks of repentance toward God and faith in our Lord Jesus Christ."
>
> —Acts 20:17–21

What is Paul's attitude and what did he experience?

What did he teach? Where did he teach?

Whom did he teach?

What was his testimony about?

"And now, behold, bound in spirit, I am on my way to Jerusalem, not knowing what will happen to me there, except that the Holy Spirit solemnly testifies to me in every city, saying that bonds and afflictions await me. But I do not consider my life of any account as dear to myself, so that I may finish my course and the ministry which I received from the Lord Jesus, to testify solemnly of the gospel of the grace of God. And now, behold, I know that all of you, among whom I went about preaching the kingdom, will no longer see my face."

—Acts 20:22–25

What is his attitude?

Where is he going? What will happen to him?

What is his purpose?

What did he preach to them? Will he see them again?

"Therefore, I testify to you this day that I am innocent of the blood of all men. For I did not shrink from declaring to you the whole purpose of God."

—Acts 20:26–27

How can he be innocent of the blood of all men?

What did he teach them?

"Be on guard for yourselves and for all the flock, among which the Holy Spirit has made you overseers, to shepherd the church of God which He purchased with His own blood. I know that after my departure savage wolves will come in among you, not sparing the flock; and from among your own selves men will arise, speaking perverse things, to draw away the disciples after them. Therefore be on the alert, remembering that night and day for a period of three years I did not cease to admonish each one with tears."

—Acts 20:28–31

What is his warning? Why? What does he know will happen?

From where will these wolves come? From where will those who speak perverse things come?

"And now I commend you to God and to the word of His grace, which is able to build you up and to give you the inheritance among all those who are sanctified."
—Acts 20:32

What is his recommendation? What is the Word able to do?

All Scripture is inspired by God and profitable for teaching, for reproof, for correction, for training in righteousness; so that the man of God may be adequate, equipped for every good work.
—2 Timothy 3:16–17

List the four things the Word is profitable for. Why?

WORD STUDY

The Greek word for "correction" is *epanorthosis*, meaning "a straightening up again, (figuratively) rectification (reformation), correction."

The Greek word for "training" is *paideia*, meaning "tutorage; i.e., education or training; by implication, disciplinary correction, chastening, chastisement, instruction, nurture."

The Word will teach us, revealing to us what is wrong and showing us how to straighten up or correct the wrong, then training us, educating us, and/or nurturing us in the right way. What then has to be the result?

Whom is he talking about that will be adequate and equipped?

For what will he be equipped?

What kind of work will it be?

How much of the work will be good?

Let the Word Dwell Richly

What is the criterion for every work being a good work?

If every work can be a good work, why aren't all the works of all believers good works?

Could this be the reason?

For the word of God is living and active and sharper than any two-edged sword, and piercing as far as the division of soul and spirit, of both joints and marrow, and able to judge the thoughts and intentions of the heart. And there is no creature hidden from His sight, but all things are open and laid bare to the eyes of Him with whom we have to do.
—Hebrews 4:12–13

What will the Word do?

Could the impact of the Word of God be painful? Is it internal or external? It seems to reach every area: the spiritual, mental, emotional, and physical, but what a cleansing when it is done! What freedom can be realized by the person who desires the sincere milk of the Word, who longs to have his senses trained by the word of righteousness to discern good and evil.

Who is hidden?

WORD STUDY

The Greek word for "laid bare" is *gumnos*, meaning "of uncertain affinity; nude (absolute or relative, literal or figurative), naked."

The Word of God is so invasive, all of our "stuff" is exposed. But when that happens, God provides the garments, just as He did for Adam and Eve in the garden. He provides training and nurturing in righteousness (2 Timothy 3:16). He gives us His righteousness. Talk about freedom!

Read on, recording from each passage what reliance we have on the Word of God.

Forever, O Lord, Your word is settled in heaven.
—Psalm 119:89

The grass withers, the flower fades, but the word of our God stands forever.
—Isaiah 40:8

"But the word of the Lord endures forever." And this is the word which was preached to you.
—1 Peter 1:25

How long will the Word last? Has it been settled? What will you do with the Word?

Let the Word Dwell Richly

In Ephesians 6 we are told to take up the full armor of God. The last piece mentioned is the sword of the Spirit, which is the Word of God. The Greek word here for *sword* is not the long weapon we normally think of, but a short, small dagger. It is incisive; it must hit a vulnerable spot or it doesn't do any damage. In addition, the word used here is *rhema,* which means "a specific statement." So the sword of the Spirit is the specific statement of the Word that meets the specific point of temptation.

Having the sword of the Spirit is not merely owning a Bible; it's knowing the specific scriptural principles that apply to a specific point of temptation. The only way Christians will know victory is if they know the principles of the Word of God and apply them where Satan attacks, where the flesh attacks, and where the world attacks. We cannot live the Christian life without studying the Bible. If you want to be free, read, study, and obey the Word of God.

Remember, the Word of God is not man's opinion, human philosophy, or somebody's ideas. It is not a pooling of the best thoughts of the best men. It is the Word of God. As you read it and study it, the Holy Spirit teaches you the deep things of God. Your faith will rest on the power of God, not on the wisdom of men (1 Corinthians 2:5). You will come to know what you really believe. And you will be able to explain the reason for the hope that is in you.

Your growth will be directly proportionate to the amount of time and effort you put into the study of the Word and the amount of the Word you put into practice. If you want to be free, stay in the Word. Read it; study it; memorize it; meditate on it; dig for the hidden treasures, and above all, live it! **"And now I commend you to God and to the word of His grace, which is able to build you up and to give you the inheritance among all those who are sanctified" (Acts 20:32).**

Is there any reason you cannot live in the freedom that Christ provides? Is there any reason you cannot depend on the influence of the Spirit in your life? Is there any reason you cannot rely on His Word? If you can think of a reason, write it down.

Chapter Thirty-Three

FREEDOM ASSURED

If the truth sets you free, and the Word is truth (Jesus said, "I am the way, the truth, and the life" in John 14:6.) and if the Word teaches us, reveals to us our wrongs, shows us how to straighten or correct the wrongs, and then helps us to live right, how does faith fit in?

Faith says, "Do it," whether you understand it or not. Faith must tie into doing or there is no faith. As James 2:26 says, faith without works is dead.

When Abraham offered Isaac, his faith was working with his works (obeying what God told him to do). As a result his faith was perfected (James 2:22).

"Without faith it is impossible to please God" (Hebrews 11:6). If we are not applying our faith to the Word we know, we are not pleasing God. In spite of all the Word we've read, all the sermons we've heard, and all that Jesus has done for us on the cross, we are not truly free until we apply faith; i.e., doing God's will whether or not we understand it, doing what the Word says just because it says it.

Freedom comes when we believe all that Jesus did on Calvary, with all it ramifications. The Word teaches us and shows us what to do. Appropriate it!

This is the same message God sent by Moses to Pharaoh: ***"Let My People Go!"*** What or who is keeping you from freedom? Whether it is a salvation issue or a specific area that has you bound, take the truth of God's Word, apply faith, and watch freedom happen.

Let's look at what happened when a synagogue official went to see Jesus about his daughter. Look for how the Word is given and applied, and look for freedom happening.

> When Jesus had crossed over again in the boat to the other side, a large crowd gathered around Him; and so He stayed by the seashore. One of the synagogue officials named Jairus came up, and on seeing Him, fell at His feet and implored Him earnestly, saying, "My little daughter is at the point of death; please come and lay Your hands on her, so that she will get well and live." And He went off with him; and a large crowd was following Him and pressing in on Him.
> —Mark 5:21–24

Where is Jesus and who is with Him?

Who is Jairus and what is his concern?

How does he approach Jesus?

Jairus is the ruler of the synagogue, a very important position in that day, but he has a problem, so he comes to Jesus. The gospel of Matthew says that after Jairus made his request, Jesus followed him. So Jesus is following Jairus and the crowd is following Jesus. Jairus' faith is moving Jesus! Read how Luke shares the same account.

> And there came a man named Jairus, and he was an official of the synagogue; and he fell at Jesus' feet, and began to implore Him to come to his house; for he had an only daughter, about twelve years old, and she was dying. But as He went, the crowds were pressing against Him.
> —Luke 8:41–42

Freedom Assured

Add any new information you see about Jairus.

What more do you learn about his daughter?

Jesus was on His way to Jairus' house when all of a sudden a woman with an issue of blood slipped up behind Him to touch the hem of His garment. She had heard there was a man in town who was healing. This woman had wrestled with her medical problem for twelve years. She had spent all her money going to doctors but was not any better. In fact, her condition had grown worse.

According to the law, she was considered unclean. That meant she could not touch anyone: husband, children or friends. She could not touch anything without it also becoming unclean. She could not even go to worship. How could she even be in this crowd, touching and pressing people? How dared she think of touching Jesus or even His garment? Why didn't she just ask Him to heal her from a distance? Perhaps she didn't want to interrupt or be pointed out.

She moved into position, hoping to touch Jesus' garment. She believed (she had heard, and faith comes by hearing) that if she could just touch His garment, she would be healed. And she was right.

Jesus, realizing someone had touched Him, wanted to know who. At this point being unclean was not the issue; He'd felt power go out of Him. The disciples could not believe He had asked such a question with a huge crowd around Him.

Everyone stopped when Jesus acknowledged that something had happened. The woman admitted who she was, and Jesus said to her, "Daughter, your faith has made you well; go in peace and be healed of your affliction" (Mark 5:34).

Daughter? What was that all about? Did you see that freedom kick in?

A little interruption became an opportunity to see faith in action. This woman did not even ask. The power of God seems to have moved automatically as she diligently sought Jesus. Notwithstanding the length of her illness, the circumstances, the risk, the people, or the disciples, active faith worked. It stopped Jesus in His tracks. Works worked with her faith and her faith was perfected. A word was heard; she believed it and moved on it. The result? She was healed.

You must believe that He is (exists) and that He is a rewarder of those who diligently seek Him (Hebrews 11:6). She did. And He did! You can. He will!

Why can't we simply believe what God says and act on it? Are we waiting for approval or agreement from someone else? If we see it in the Scriptures, we can believe it and do it. Why wait until someone else preaches it, teaches it, or says it the same way God did? No wonder we are not stopping God in His tracks with our faith. No wonder we do not have all the rewards and the goodness that God has stored up for us, the saints.

Are you exhibiting amazing faith? When you hear the Word, do you believe it and move on it? Are you diligently seeking God?

How has this woman helped you understand something about faith? Record it and move on it. It will change our life.

Chapter Thirty-Four

HIGH RATE OF RETURN

What was Jairus doing while Jesus was talking to the woman who was healed of the issue of blood? It is not recorded that he uttered a word, mumbled a complaint, or tried to pull rank. Was he patiently waiting, knowing his daughter was at home sick and dying?

As Jesus says the last words to the healed, faith-exercising woman, people from Jairus' house approach.

> While He was still speaking, they came from the house of the synagogue official, saying, "Your daughter has died; why trouble the Teacher anymore?" But Jesus, overhearing what was being spoken, said to the synagogue official, "Do not be afraid any longer, only believe."
> —Mark 5:35–36

What has happened? What is their recommendation?

What does Jesus say? To whom does He speak? Who else?

WORD STUDY

The Greek word for "trouble" is *skullo,* meaning "to flay; i.e. (figuratively), to harass, trouble."

When Jesus says, "Do not be afraid, only believe," He is speaking two present imperatives. In the Greek construction that means they are commands, and they are continuous or repeated actions. Jesus commands Jairus not to be afraid *any longer* and to *continue* to believe Him.

As soon as the people speak, Jesus comes right back with His words. He gives Jairus unfailing words, encouraging words, life-giving words in an otherwise hopeless situation.

But another word has been spoken in Jairus' ear. A word from the people that leads him to believe them, to believe based on the circumstances, to believe that it is too late.

The crowd just saw what happened to a woman who had a twelve-year-old problem, and Jesus is headed to solve the problem of a twelve-year-old. But the folks say, "Why bother?"

Whenever we are in trouble, we can go to Jesus. We are never a bother to Him. He does not feel like we are harassing Him.

Jairus could stand on what the people were saying or he could continue to believe what Jesus was telling him. But he had to make a choice.

> And He allowed no one to accompany Him, except Peter and James and John the brother of James. They came to the house of the synagogue official; and He saw a commotion, and people loudly weeping and wailing. And entering in, He said to them, "Why make a commotion and weep? The child has not died, but is asleep." They began laughing at Him. But putting them all out, He took along the child's father and mother and His own companions, and entered the room where the child was.
>
> —Mark 5:37–40

High Rate of Return

What does Jesus do and why?

When they reach the house, what do they find? What are they doing and why? Has Jesus led Jairus astray?

In that day, when someone died or was nearing death, paid mourners would come to weep and wail and cause a great disturbance. As Jairus approaches, he does not say a word. What could he be thinking? What conclusions did he probably draw in his mind?

What does Jesus say to the people, for all to hear? What do the weeping, wailing people begin to do?

What does Jesus do to them?

WORD STUDY

The Greek word for "laugh" is *katagelao,* meaning "to laugh down; i.e., deride, laugh to scorn."

The Greek word for "put out" is *ekballo,* meaning "to eject (literally or figuratively), bring forth, cast (forth, out), drive (out), expel, leave, pluck (pull, take, thrust) out, put forth (out), send away (forth, out). To cast, throw, drive. To cast, throw out." This is the same word used in Mark 1:12, when the Spirit drives Jesus into the wilderness to be tempted. It is the same word that is spoken of demons, to cast or drive out, to expel from the body of someone, as in Mark 6:9. Metaphorically it is used in the sense of casting out,

to scorn and reproach, to reject, as in Luke 6:22, when people falsely slander you and "say all manner of evil against you falsely" (Matthew 5:11).

Jesus had just gotten rid of one unbelieving crowd, and here He encounters another one. Based on what you learned in the "Word Study" above, what were they doing when they laughed at Jesus, and why did He throw them out?

Who enters the room with Him? Based on His reason for eliminating the others, why does it appear that this group is allowed to enter the room? Has Jairus made a choice between what Jesus said and what the people are saying?

Taking the child by the hand, He said to her, "Talitha kum!" (which translated means, "Little girl, I say to you, get up!"). Immediately the girl got up and began to walk, for she was twelve years old. And immediately they were completely astounded. And He gave them strict orders that no one should know about this, and He said that something should be given her to eat.
—Mark 5:41–43

They are in the room now. What does Jesus do?

What is the response from the girl? From everyone else?

High Rate of Return

Jairus had numerous obstacles in the way of believing Jesus, including his position and the voice of the people. List other obstacles he encountered from the time he first approached Jesus until he enters his daughter's room.

What obstacles keep you from believing all that Jesus says?

At what point would you say freedom happened for Jairus?

Obstacles to believing Jesus:

Jairus'   Yours

Point of freedom:

Jairus'   Yours

Therefore, let us fear if, while a promise remains of entering His rest, any one of you may seem to have come short of it. For indeed we have had good news preached to us, just as they also; but the word they heard did not profit them, because it was not united by faith in those who heard.

—Hebrews 4:1–2

What is the promise?

WORD STUDY

The Greek word for "remains" is *kataleipo*, meaning "to leave down; i.e., behind; by implication, to abandon, have remaining, to forsake, leave, reserve."

Considering what you have learned from the "Word Study," what have they done with the promise?

Why didn't the word they heard profit them?

WORD STUDY

The Greek word for "profit" is *opheleo*, meaning "to be useful; i.e., to benefit, advantage, better, prevail, profit."

Read Hebrews 4:1–2 again and the definition of *profit* in the "Word Study." How do you fit into this picture?

Deception comes in many forms, whether open or subtle. We seem to look for the newest, latest technology, state-of-the-art ideas and plans, sometimes to the detriment of what God laid out in His Word long ago. To the world, the Word of God and the things He requires may seem foolish or weak, but God chooses the things that are not in order to destroy or make void the things that are. (See 1 Corinthians 1:27–29.)

Popular religious opinions and political movements have been around a long time, but Jesus chose to follow God's kingdom. He accomplished His work with the faithful few, the remnant, and small, seemingly insignificant things.

Jairus chose to follow Jesus. So did the woman with the issue of blood. What is your choice?

Promises to the Obedient and the Disobedient

Chapter Thirty-Five

STANDING ON THE PROMISES OR HANGING AROUND THE PREMISES

What does God promise to those who are obedient to His Word? What does He say in His Word about His promises and how they relate to us?

Read the following passages and record what you see about His promises.

> For by these He has granted to us His precious and magnificent promises, so that by them you may become partakers of the divine nature, having escaped the corruption that is in the world by lust.
>
> —2 Peter 1:4

What will these promises help you escape?

> Therefore, having these promises, beloved, let us cleanse ourselves from all defilement of flesh and spirit, perfecting holiness in the fear of God.
>
> —2 Corinthians 7:1

What is the responsibility of the believer who has these promises?

Let us hold fast the confession of our hope without wavering, for He who promised is faithful.

—Hebrews 10:23

What is the responsibility of the believer? Who is faithful?

For I say that Christ has become a servant to the circumcision on behalf of the truth of God to confirm the promises given to the fathers, and for the Gentiles to glorify God for His mercy; as it is written, "Therefore I will give praise to you among the Gentiles, and I will sing to your name." Again he says, "Rejoice, O Gentiles, with his people." And again, "Praise the Lord all you Gentiles, and let all the peoples praise him." Again Isaiah says, "There shall come the root of Jesse, and he who arises to rule over the Gentiles, in him shall the Gentiles hope." Now may the God of hope fill you with all joy and peace in believing, so that you will abound in hope by the power of the Holy Spirit.

—Romans 15:8–13

What is Christ's relationship to the promises?

What two groups are being addressed?

Standing on the Promises or Hanging around the Premises

Where does our hope lie?

How does the believer abound in hope? Look carefully at verses 12 and 13 to determine who works in the believer in this area of hope and belief.

What assurance do you see in the following verse?

> God is not a man, that He should lie, Nor a son of man, that He should repent; Has He said, and will He not do it? Or has He spoken, and will He not make it good?
>
> —Numbers 23:19

Let's look at an example of this promise-keeping God.

In Exodus 32, Moses has been gone for forty days and nights, receiving the Ten Commandments from God. The people had never been separated from Moses for such a long period of time. They approached Aaron, Moses' brother, and wanted to make a god to go before them. Aaron, their high priest, suggested they take off their gold and make a golden calf. Great idea! So Aaron fashioned the calf; an altar was built, and the feast was planned. They worshipped the calf, bringing peace offerings and burnt offerings, eating, drinking, and playing before it.

God was not happy, and He talked to Moses about it.

Listen to this discussion, marking *the Lord* and all pronouns for Him, *Moses,* and *the people.*

> Then the Lord spoke to Moses, "Go down at once, for your people, whom you brought up from the land of Egypt, have corrupted themselves. They have quickly turned aside from the way which I commanded them. They have made for themselves a molten calf, and have worshiped it and have sacrificed to it and said, 'This is your god, O Israel, who brought you up from the land of Egypt!'" The Lord said to Moses, "I have seen this people, and behold, they are an obstinate people. Now then let Me alone, that My anger may burn against them and that I may destroy them; and I will make of you a great nation."
>
> —Exodus 32:7–10

What does the Lord say about the people? Looking at the definitions below, how does He describe them? Whose people are they?

WORD STUDY

The Hebrew word for "corrupt" is *shachath,* meaning "to decay, ruin (literally or figuratively), batter, cast off, corrupt, destroy, lose, mar, perish, spill, spoiler, utterly, waste."

The Hebrew word for "obstinate" is *qasheh,* meaning "churlish, cruel, grievous, hardhearted, heavy, impudent, obstinate, sore, sorrowful, stiff (necked), stubborn in trouble."

Why is God so angry? What does He say He will do to them? What does He propose to Moses?

> Then Moses entreated the Lord his God, and said, "O Lord, why does Your anger burn against Your people whom You have brought out from the land of Egypt with great power and with a mighty hand? Why should the Egyptians speak, saying, 'With evil intent He brought them out to kill them in the mountains and to destroy them from the face of the earth'? Turn from Your burning anger and change Your mind about doing harm to Your people."
> —Exodus 32:11–12

Whose people are they, according to Moses? How did God bring them out of Egypt? Whom does Moses bring into the picture? What does Moses tell God the Egyptians will do? What is the basis of Moses' appeal?

Standing on the Promises or Hanging around the Premises

> "Remember Abraham, Isaac, and Israel, Your servants to whom You swore by Yourself, and said to them, 'I will multiply your descendants as the stars of the heavens, and all this land of which I have spoken I will give to your descendants, and they shall inherit it forever.'"
>
> —Exodus 32:13

Of what does Moses remind God? What is the second basis of Moses' appeal?

God promised Abraham in Genesis 12:2 that He would make him a great nation. Can you see why Moses could not accept God's proposal in Exodus 32:7–10? Why?

> So the Lord changed His mind about the harm which He said He would do to His people.
>
> —Exodus 32:14

After Moses' double appeal, what does God do?

Moses and Joshua head down the mountain, with God's writing engraved on two tablets of stone. When they were close enough, they could hear the people. They moved closer and they could see the calf and the dancing. Moses was so angry, he threw the tablets down and broke them, burned the calf, ground it into powder, and made the people drink it. Then he confronted Aaron.

> Then Moses said to Aaron, "What did this people do to you, that you have brought such great sin upon them?" Aaron said, "Do not let the anger of my lord burn; you know the people yourself, that they are prone to evil." For they said to me, 'Make a god for us who will go before us; for this Moses, the man who brought us up from the land of Egypt, we do not know what has become of him.' "I said to them, 'Whoever has any gold, let them tear it off.' So they gave it to me, and I threw it into the fire, and out came this calf."
>
> —Exodus 32:21–24

How does Aaron respond to Moses' confrontation? How does Aaron describe the making of the calf? Does he take ownership?

By this time the people are out of control. Moses has to take disciplinary action. He calls for repentance. He calls for all those who are on the Lord's side to join him. The sons of Levi were to kill every man who was not on the Lord's side. Three thousand men were killed that day. The evil was purged from the camp so they could be blessed.

The next day Moses went before the Lord to make atonement for the people. He asked the Lord to forgive the people, and if He could not, to blot his name out of the book of life. Moses' first prayer reminded God of His reputation and of His covenant. But this prayer does not line up with God's promise at all. No man could take the punishment for another. God had said that everyone shall be put to death for his own sin.

God told Moses to lead the people where He told him to go. God said His angel would go with them. But He also said He would punish them for their sin and would smite the people because of the calf that Aaron had made. God keeps His promises to the obedient and to the disobedient.

Is this a good time to repent? We will continue to look at how God keeps His promises in the next chapter.

Chapter Thirty-Six

MY PRESENCE WILL GO WITH YOU

Moses caught what God said about sending an angel with them. Did that mean God was not going too? These are His people; why would He not go with them?

> Then the Lord spoke to Moses, "Depart, go up from here, you and the people whom you have brought up from the land of Egypt, to the land of which I swore to Abraham, Isaac, and Jacob, saying, 'To your descendants I will give it.' "I will send an angel before you and I will drive out the Canaanite, the Amorite, the Hittite, the Perizzite, the Hivite and the Jebusite. Go up to a land flowing with milk and honey; for I will not go up in your midst, because you are an obstinate people, and I might destroy you on the way." When the people heard this sad word, they went into mourning, and none of them put on his ornaments. For the Lord had said to Moses, Say to the sons of Israel, 'You are an obstinate people; should I go up in your midst for one moment, I would destroy you. Now therefore, put off your ornaments from you, that I may know what I shall do with you.'"
>
> —Exodus 33:1–5

What is God's instruction to Moses? Who is He going to send with him?

What does God say about the people? Why does God say He is not going?

What is the reaction of the people?

Read on and describe how the Lord used to speak to Moses.

Thus the Lord used to speak to Moses face to face, just as a man speaks to his friend. When Moses returned to the camp, his servant Joshua, the son of Nun, a young man, would not depart from the tent.

—Exodus 33:11

God speaks to Moses as a friend and Moses speaks in a plain yet reverent manner to God.

Then Moses said to the Lord, "See, You say to me, 'Bring up this people!' But You Yourself have not let me know whom You will send with me. Moreover, You have said, 'I have known you by name, and you have also found favor in My sight.' Now therefore, I pray You, if I have found favor in Your sight, let me know Your ways that I may know You, so that I may find favor in Your sight. Consider too, that this nation is Your people."

—Exodus 33:12–13

My Presence Will Go with You

What is Moses' concern?

How does Moses say that God describes him?

WORD STUDY

The Hebrew word for "favor" is *chen*, meaning "graciousness, i.e. subjective (kindness, favor) or objective (beauty), favour, pleasant, precious, (well-) favoured."

What does Moses want to know about God? Why?

And He said, "My presence shall go with you, and I will give you rest." Then he said to Him, "If Your presence does not go with us, do not lead us up from here. For how then can it be known that I have found favor in Your sight, I and Your people? Is it not by Your going with us, so that we, I and Your people, may be distinguished from all the other people who are upon the face of the earth?"

—Exodus 33:14–16

What is God's response?

As if Moses does not hear God, he continues with his argument to convince God that He should go with them. Is this not wonderful? Moses prays to God and we see His immediate response. List the points of his argument.

The Lord said to Moses, "I will also do this thing of which you have spoken; for you have found favor in My sight and I have known you by name." Then Moses said, "I pray You, show me Your glory!"

—Exodus 33:17–18

What is the Lord's response?

Moses is not one to quit. He takes the discussion further, even though God has said at least two times in this discussion that He will go. What does he ask God to show him now?

WORD STUDY

The Hebrew word for "glory" is *kabowd*, meaning "properly, weight, but only figuratively in a good sense, splendor or copiousness, glorious, gloriously, glory, honour, honourable. It means weight, honor, esteem, glory, majesty; abundance, wealth." (See Genesis 31:1; 1 Kings 8:11; Malachi 1:6.) Poetically, it can refer to a soul or a person (Psalm 30:12).

Moses has heretofore heard the voice of God in a cloud and in the fire. He has experienced the miracles and plagues of God. He has interacted with God to bring the sons of Israel out of Egypt and from under the hand of Pharaoh. He saw the effect of God as He thundered in the mountain prior to the giving of the Ten Commandments. He saw God as I AM when he asked, "Who shall I say sent me?" He saw God as Jehovah Rapha when He healed the waters of Marah, and as Jehovah Nissi when He delivered them from the hands of Amalek. Now Moses is having an intimate conversation with God and he wants more, a closer look, a deeper relationship. "If in fact I am precious to You," he says, "if I have found favor with You, show me Your ways. Don't send us, go with us. Come closer and show me Your glory!"

My Presence Will Go with You

He wants to see God's glory, that which seems to be the depths of His being. In light of what is going on, Moses does not seem to be asking just for himself; he seems to be concerned about the people and how God responds to them as well. If the people are to be distinguished from all other nations, it can only happen if God is with them. The other nations can only know who God is if He goes with them always.

> And He said, "I Myself will make all My goodness pass before you, and will proclaim the name of the Lord before you; and I will be gracious to whom I will be gracious, and will show compassion on whom I will show compassion." But He said, "You cannot see My face, for no man can see Me and live!"
>
> —Exodus 33:19–20

How does God respond to Moses' request? What two things does He promise Moses?

If God's name is His nature, His character, and a reflection of all His attributes and all that He is, what is the Lord planning to show Moses? Consider the meaning for goodness (see "Word Study" below) to determine what Moses will see as God goes with them.

WORD STUDY

The Hebrew word for "goodness" is *tuwb*, meaning "good (as a noun), in the widest sense, especially goodness (superlative concretely, the best), beauty, gladness, welfare, fair, gladness, good (-ness, thing, -s), joy, go well with."

The Hebrew word for "gracious" is *chanan*, meaning "properly, to bend or stoop in kindness to an inferior; to favor, bestow; causatively to implore (i.e. move to favor by petition), to beseech, fair, (be, find, shew) favour (-able), be (deal, give, grant (gracious-ly), intreat, (be) merciful, have (shew) mercy (on, upon), have pity upon."

The Hebrew word for "compassion" is *racham*, meaning "to fondle; by implication, to love, especially to compassionate, have compassion (on, upon), love, (find, have, obtain, shew) mercy."

When He speaks of having compassion and being gracious (look at the definitions above), whom is God talking about? What started this discussion in the first place? Put that all together and record what you believe God is telling Moses.

Then the Lord said, "Behold, there is a place by Me, and you shall stand there on the rock; and it will come about, while My glory is passing by, that I will put you in the cleft of the rock and cover you with My hand until I have passed by. Then I will take My hand away and you shall see My back, but My face shall not be seen."

—Exodus 33:21–23

What instructions do you see for Moses?

List the promises of God that you see in these verses.

Where will Moses be when God's glory moves? Do you wonder how Moses can stand on the rock and be in the cleft of the rock at the same time?

Let's study a few cross-references on the rock. Look at what David writes in Psalm 27.

My Presence Will Go with You

For in the day of trouble He will conceal me in His tabernacle; in the secret place of His tent He will hide me; He will lift me up on a rock. And now my head will be lifted up above my enemies around me, and I will offer in His tent sacrifices with shouts of joy; I will sing, yes, I will sing praises to the Lord.

—Psalm 27:5–6

What time is it? Record what you see about the rock. What results do you see?

He who dwells in the shelter of the Most High Will abide in the shadow of the Almighty. I will say to the Lord, "My refuge and my fortress, My God, in whom I trust!" For it is He who delivers you from the snare of the trapper And from the deadly pestilence. He will cover you with His pinions, And under His wings you may seek refuge; His faithfulness is a shield and bulwark.

—Psalm 91:1–4

Where is he dwelling? What does God provide? How is God described?

Compare Exodus 17 with 1 Corinthians 10, looking for information about the rock.

Then the Lord said to Moses, "Pass before the people and take with you some of the elders of Israel; and take in your hand your staff with which you struck the Nile, and go. Behold, I will stand before you there on the rock at Horeb; and you shall strike the rock, and water will come out of it, that the people may drink." And Moses did so in the sight of the elders of Israel.

—Exodus 17:5–6

For I do not want you to be unaware, brethren, that our fathers were all under the cloud and all passed through the sea; and all were baptized into Moses in the cloud and in the sea; and all ate the same spiritual food; and all drank the same spiritual drink, for they were drinking from a spiritual rock which followed them; and the rock was Christ.

—1 Corinthians 10:1–4

Did you know that Mount Horeb and Mount Sinai are the same? In Exodus 17, where is the rock? In 1 Corinthians 10, who is the rock that followed them?

Read what John says as he describes Jesus.

> For of His fullness we have all received, and grace upon grace. For the Law was given through Moses; grace and truth were realized through Jesus Christ. No one has seen God at any time; the only begotten God who is in the bosom of the Father, He has explained Him.
> —John 1:16–18

Record what John says about Jesus.

Who explains whom in John 1:16–18? Do you see any relationship to what we have studied in Exodus 33?

> Now the Lord said to Moses, "Cut out for yourself two stone tablets like the former ones, and I will write on the tablets the words that were on the former tablets which you shattered. So be ready by morning, and come up in the morning to Mount Sinai, and present yourself there to Me on the top of the mountain. No man is to come up with you, nor let any man be seen anywhere on the mountain; even the flocks and the herds may not graze in front of that mountain." So he cut out two stone tablets like the former ones, and Moses rose up early in the morning and went up to Mount Sinai, as the Lord had commanded him, and he took two stone tablets in his hand. The Lord descended in the cloud and stood there with him as he called upon the name of the Lord.
> —Exodus 34:1–5

My Presence Will Go with You

Where is Moses to go and whom should he take with him? What is the other name for this mountain?

What is Moses doing and who is with him? Compare this passage with Exodus 33:21.

Then the Lord passed by in front of him and proclaimed, "The Lord, the Lord God, compassionate and gracious, slow to anger, and abounding in lovingkindness and truth; who keeps lovingkindness for thousands, who forgives iniquity, transgression and sin; yet He will by no means leave the guilty unpunished, visiting the iniquity of fathers on the children and on the grandchildren to the third and fourth generations." Moses made haste to bow low toward the earth and worship. He said, "If now I have found favor in Your sight, O Lord, I pray, let the Lord go along in our midst, even though the people are so obstinate, and pardon our iniquity and our sin, and take us as Your own possession."

—Exodus 34:6–9

Look at God fulfilling His promise to stand with Moses. What other promises are realized in Exodus 33:19–20?

Of what else does God remind Moses in Exodus 34:6–9 and what is Moses' response?

What three things does Moses ask God again, and who does he specifically bring into the picture?

What does he ask God to pardon? Did you notice he includes himself in the sin? Remember, this is still the golden-calf issue.

Then God said, "Behold, I am going to make a covenant. Before all your people I will perform miracles which have not been produced in all the earth nor among any of the nations; and all the people among whom you live will see the working of the Lord, for it is a fearful thing that I am going to perform with you."

—Exodus 34:10

Of what does the covenant consist? What will God do? Who will see it?

"Be sure to observe what I am commanding you this day: behold, I am going to drive out the Amorite before you, and the Canaanite, the Hittite, the Perizzite, the Hivite and the Jebusite. Watch yourself that you make no covenant with the inhabitants of the land into which you are going, or it will become a snare in your midst."

—Exodus 34:11–12

What is God going to do? What are they to do?

My Presence Will Go with You

> But rather, you are to tear down their altars and smash their sacred pillars and cut down their Asherim—for you shall not worship any other god, for the Lord, whose name is Jealous, is a jealous God—otherwise you might make a covenant with the inhabitants of the land and they would play the harlot with their gods and sacrifice to their gods, and someone might invite you to eat of his sacrifice, and you might take some of his daughters for your sons, and his daughters might play the harlot with their gods and cause your sons also to play the harlot with their gods. You shall make for yourself no molten gods.
> —Exodus 34:13–17

What is Israel to do? Why?

What name of God is made known here? Why?

Israel broke the covenant with God by worshipping the golden calf. Here God makes reconciliation, restores them, and seems to elevate them to an even higher position. He had made a covenant with Abraham centuries ago that He would make them a great nation, and that all the nations of the world would be blessed through them. As God re-establishes His covenant with this generation, He seems to be looking back at the covenant made long ago with Abraham. One thing you can be sure of about God: He will always keep His promises.

> For the Son of God, Christ Jesus, who was preached among you by us—by me and Silvanus and Timothy—was not yes and no, but is yes in Him. For as many as are the promises of God, in Him they are yes; therefore also through Him is our Amen to the glory of God through us.
> —2 Corinthians 1:19–20

What is the answer to every promise of God? Who gives the answer? How is the answer made known? Who gets the glory?

Every promise of God is sure, every promise is positive, and every promise is absolutely guaranteed. The yes is in Jesus and the amen is through Jesus, but the promises are worked through the believers.

What promise have you been reciting, have even memorized, but are not really realizing the total benefit of? When you yield to His will, God's promises become real.

Chapter Thirty-Seven
___

Promises Guaranteed

Jehoshaphat was the king of Israel and he was in trouble. It was the kind of trouble that could destroy life or at least result in bondage for him and all of Judah. As we read this story, think of promises that would be helpful to him or promises you would cling to if you were in this kind of trouble.

> Now it came about after this that the sons of Moab and the sons of Ammon, together with some of the Meunites, came to make war against Jehoshaphat. Then some came and reported to Jehoshaphat, saying, "A great multitude is coming against you from beyond the sea, out of Aram and behold, they are in Hazazon-tamar (that is Engedi)."
> —2 Chronicles 20:1–2

Describe the trouble and the extent of it.

Moab and Ammon are the descendants of Lot as a result of an incestuous relationship with his daughters. Lot was Abraham's nephew. So these are distant relatives. Nothing like a family feud!

> Jehoshaphat was afraid and turned his attention to seek the Lord, and proclaimed a fast throughout all Judah. So Judah gathered together to seek help from the Lord; they even came from all the cities of Judah to seek the Lord.
> —2 Chronicles 20:3–4

List Jehoshaphat's first three reactions.

List promises you would cling to in this situation (for example, "Pray and not faint").
You can pull the promises from your memory, your Bible, or the promise list in the appendix. This will help you in the days to come.
Promises to cling to:

> Then Jehoshaphat stood in the assembly of Judah and Jerusalem, in the house of the Lord before the new court, and he said, "O Lord, the God of our fathers, are You not God in the heavens? And are You not ruler over all the kingdoms of the nations? Power and might are in Your hand so that no one can stand against You. Did You not, O our God, drive out the inhabitants of this land before Your people Israel and give it to the descendants of Abraham Your friend forever? They have lived in it, and have built You a sanctuary there for Your name, saying, 'Should evil come upon us, the sword, or judgment, or pestilence, or famine, we will stand before this house and before You (for Your name is in this house) and cry to You in our distress, and You will hear and deliver us.'"
> —2 Chronicles 20:5–9

Look at how Jehoshaphat acknowledges who God is in verse 6.

Promises Guaranteed

In Genesis 12, God promised the land to Abraham and all his descendants. He makes a covenant with Abraham. What does Jehoshaphat say about Abraham? Why would he mention Abraham in his prayer?

Add to your promise list.

More promises to cling to:

Now behold, the sons of Ammon and Moab and Mount Seir, whom You did not let Israel invade when they came out of the land of Egypt (they turned aside from them and did not destroy them), see how they are rewarding us by coming to drive us out from Your possession which You have given us as an inheritance.
—2 Chronicles 20:10–11

In the past, what had God forbidden Israel to do to these enemies?

What is Jehoshaphat's concern now? List promises from this passage.

More promises to cling to:

"O our God, will You not judge them? For we are powerless before this great multitude who are coming against us; nor do we know what to do, but our eyes are on You. All Judah was standing before the Lord, with their infants, their wives and their children."

—2 Chronicles 20:12–13

The king is praying. What does he admit? Who is there?
Promises to cling to:

Then in the midst of the assembly the Spirit of the Lord came upon Jahaziel the son of Zechariah, the son of Benaiah, the son of Jeiel, the son of Mattaniah, the Levite of the sons of Asaph; and he said, "Listen, all Judah and the inhabitants of Jerusalem and King Jehoshaphat: thus says the Lord to you, 'Do not fear or be dismayed because of this great multitude, for the battle is not yours but God's.'"

—2 Chronicles 20:14–15

What does God promise to them?

What instruction does He give them?

Promises Guaranteed

Whose battle is this?

Promises you can cling to:

"Tomorrow go down against them. Behold, they will come up by the ascent of Ziz, and you will find them at the end of the valley in front of the wilderness of Jeruel. You need not fight in this battle; station yourselves, stand and see the salvation of the Lord on your behalf, O Judah and Jerusalem. Do not fear or be dismayed; tomorrow go out to face them, for the Lord is with you."

—2 Chronicles 20:16–17

What are God's instructions?

What does He tell them to watch for?

What are they to do when they find them? What is God's promise?

Promises to cling to:

Jehoshaphat bowed his head with his face to the ground, and all Judah and the inhabitants of Jerusalem fell down before the Lord, worshiping the Lord. The Levites, from the sons of the Kohathites and of the sons of the Korahites, stood up to praise the Lord God of Israel, with a very loud voice. They rose early in the morning and went out to the wilderness of Tekoa; and when they went out, Jehoshaphat stood and said, "Listen to me, O Judah and inhabitants of Jerusalem, put your trust in the Lord your God and you will be established. Put your trust in His prophets and succeed." When he had consulted with the people, he appointed those who sang to the Lord and those who praised Him in holy attire, as they went out before the army and said, "Give thanks to the Lord, for His lovingkindness is everlasting."

—2 Chronicles 20:18–21

What is their response?

In whom are they to trust? What will happen if they do?

What did they say about the Lord?

Promises Guaranteed

Don't you love it? They are in the same situation, the enemies are still pursuing, but they are standing on the promises of God. They worship, they praise, and they do it all with a very loud voice. They can't just worship, sing, and praise; they have to trust God and the word he sent in order to be established and to succeed.

Promises to cling to:

> When they began singing and praising, the Lord set ambushes against the sons of Ammon, Moab and Mount Seir, who had come against Judah; so they were routed. For the sons of Ammon and Moab rose up against the inhabitants of Mount Seir destroying them completely; and when they had finished with the inhabitants of Seir, they helped to destroy one another. When Judah came to the lookout of the wilderness, they looked toward the multitude, and behold, they were corpses lying on the ground, and no one had escaped. When Jehoshaphat and his people came to take their spoil, they found much among them, including goods, garments and valuable things which they took for themselves, more than they could carry. And they were three days taking the spoil because there was so much.
> —2 Chronicles 20:22–25

What happened to their enemies? How many got away?

What was the extra added benefit?

Promises to cling to:

Then on the fourth day they assembled in the valley of Beracah, for there they blessed the Lord. Therefore they have named that place "The Valley of Beracah" until today. Every man of Judah and Jerusalem returned with Jehoshaphat at their head, returning to Jerusalem with joy, for the Lord had made them to rejoice over their enemies. They came to Jerusalem with harps, lyres and trumpets to the house of the Lord. And the dread of God was on all the kingdoms of the lands when they heard that the Lord had fought against the enemies of Israel. So the kingdom of Jehoshaphat was at peace, for his God gave him rest on all sides.
—2 Chronicles 20:26–30

In the passage above, what benefits does God give them?

List promises to cling to:

When trouble came, the king's initial response was fear, but that didn't last long. He turned to God, and he called all those in the line of fire to fast. He prayed the promises of God. The focus was on God, His power, His might, His promises, and His covenant. The king acknowledged that he was powerless, that he did not know what to do, but that he was going to focus on God. He stood on the promises of God!

And God responds, big time. He says, "I have you covered. I'll fight for you. In fact, this is not even your fight, although you will have to face the enemy." Their responsibility was not to fear, not to be dismayed, but to stand still and watch God deliver them. This was His fight.

They worshipped and praised God with loud shouts of "Give thanks to the Lord for His lovingkindness is everlasting!" They did not wait until the battle was over to worship and praise God. Genuine praise and worship cannot come without genuine trust and belief in God and

His Word. They were dressed for the part, in holy attire, as they offered up praise to God in the midst of trouble.

The conclusion of the matter was just as God promised: He delivered them! But that was not all. No one can go after God's people who believe Him and trust Him and get away with it. As they continued to praise Him, He blessed them with the spoils, gave them joy, put the fear of God on all the kingdoms around them, and gave them peace. All they asked for was to get out of trouble, out of a would-be bondage situation, and God did exceeding abundantly above all they could ask or think (Ephesians 3:20). He *really* is a rewarder of those who diligently seek Him!

Sound simple? Well it's easier than you think. The ways of the Lord are not hard (1 John 5:3). He has made all the provisions for you to live in the freedom He provides. God wants His people to be free; that is why He sent Jesus.

When God told Moses to tell Pharaoh to **"*Let My people go,*"** Pharaoh didn't want to; he had to. When God manifested Himself in the form of man, and Jesus came to set the captives free, He had to and He did! He came to give a garland instead of ashes, gladness instead of mourning, and a garment of praise instead of a spirit of fainting. He did it all so His people could be called oaks of righteousness, the planting of the Lord, so that He may be glorified (Isaiah 61:3).

God's people have been set free. But if you are not living in freedom, not receiving all that God desires to give, you are cheating yourself or allowing someone else to cheat you. As Paul admonished the Corinthians, "I urge you, child of God, not to receive the grace of God in vain. Give no cause for offense, in order that the ministry will not be discredited" (2 Corinthians 6:1–3). Glorify God in all you do, and commend yourself as a servants of God. You have been set free, so live free! His message is…

"Let My People Go!"

Appendix

Plan of Salvation

> These things I have written to you who believe in the name of the Son of God, in order that you may know that you have eternal life.
>
> —1 John 5:13

How can you know if you have eternal life? Do church attendance, ministry work, baptism, growing up in a Christian home, or being a good person mean you are saved? No!

HOW DO YOU KNOW?

The Word of God says if you have the Son you have life (1 John 5:11–12) and you can know that you know Him if you keep His commands (1 John 2:2–3). Your life, your consistent practice of His Word, is the proof.

Follow the instructions below to see how the Word describes those "born of God." Do you line up with His Word?

1. Read 1 John (all five chapters).
2. Mark (underline or circle) every occurrence of *born, God, know,* or *known*.
3. Make a list of what you discover about those "born of God" and what you can "know" in the spaces provided below.

Born of God

1 John 2:29 _____

1 John 3:9–10 _____

1 John 4:7–8 _____

1 John 5:1 _____

1 John 5:4 _____

I John 5:18 _____

What You Can Know

1 John 2:3–4 _____

1 John 2:11 _____

1 John 3:1–2 _____

1 John 3:5–6 _____

1 John 3:14–16 _____

1 John 3:19 _____

1 John 3:22–24 _____

1 John 4:2 _____

1 John 4:6 _____

1 John 4:8 _____

1 John 4:13 _____

1 John 4:16 _____

1 John 5:2 _____

1 John 5:14–16 _____

1 John 5:18–20 _____

Appendix

ABSOLUTELY SURE

Now that you see God's description of those "born of God" and you've made a list of what you can "know," are you absolutely sure that you are saved? If so, praise the Lord! If not, and you want to be saved, please read on.

1. Believe you are a sinner.

For all have sinned and fall short of the glory of God.

—Romans 3:23

2. Believe you deserve to go to hell.

Therefore, just as through one man sin entered into the world, and death through sin, and so death spread to all men, because all sinned.

—Romans 5:12

3. Believe Jesus died to pay for your sins.

But God demonstrates His own love toward us, in that while we were yet sinners, Christ died for us.

—Romans 5:8

4. Believe you need to repent, a change of heart, mind and direction

The Lord is not slow about His promise, as some count slowness, but is patient toward you, not wishing for any to perish but for all to come to repentance.

—2 Peter 3:9

5. Trust Jesus as your Lord and Savior.

If you confess with your mouth Jesus as Lord, and believe in your heart that God raised Him from the dead, you shall be saved; for with the heart man believes, resulting in righteousness, and with the mouth he confesses, resulting in salvation. For the Scripture says, "Whoever will call upon the name of the Lord will be saved."

—Romans 10:9–13

Now is the time to make your decision. Now is the accepted time. Now is the day of salvation!

—2 Corinthians 6:2

Plan for Growth

Now that you are saved…grow in grace.

You therefore, beloved, knowing this beforehand, be on your guard so that you are not carried away by the error of unprincipled men and fall from your own steadfastness, but grow in the grace and knowledge of our Lord and Savior Jesus Christ. To Him be the glory, both now and to the day of eternity. Amen.

—2 Peter 3:17–18

HOW TO GROW SPIRITUALLY

Therefore if anyone is in Christ, he is a new creature; the old things passed away; behold, new things have come.

—2 Corinthians 5:17

Look up the Scriptures listed below and discover through God's Word how to grow in grace and in the knowledge of our Lord and Savior, Jesus Christ.

Know that God Is Sovereign

Numbers 23:19 _____

Daniel 4:35 _____

John 1:1 _____

Know What to Do First

Matthew 6:33 _____

Matthew 11:28–30 _____

2 Timothy 2:15 _____

Know What Pleases God

1 Samuel 15:22 _____

Colossians 1:10 _____

Hebrews 11:6 _____

1 Peter 1:15–16 _____

Appendix

Know the Righteous Way

Make a list of how the righteous live:

2 Timothy 3:16–17 _____
Galatians 2:20 _____
Ephesians 4:22–32 _____

Examine an example of growing in grace:

Acts 26:9–18 _____

Know What Work Must Be Done

Matthew 5:16 _____
1 Corinthians 12:4, 11 _____
2 Corinthians 5:18–20 _____
Ephesians 2:10 _____

Know How to Do the Work

Philippians 2:12–13 _____
Philippians 4:13 _____

Know What God Says about Giving

Psalm 116:12 _____
Luke 6:38 _____
2 Corinthians 9:6–7 _____
Galatians 6:6–8 _____

Know How to Keep in Touch with God

Luke 18:1 _____
John 15:7–8 _____
Philippians 4:6–7 _____
1 John 5:14–15 _____

Romans 8:35–39 _____

Philippians 1:6 _____

Know What to Do If You Sin

Proverbs 28:13 _____

1 John 2:1 _____

But thanks be to God, who gives us the victory through our Lord Jesus Christ. Therefore, my beloved brethren, be steadfast, immovable, always abounding in the work of the Lord, knowing that your toil is not in vain in the Lord.

—1 Corinthians 15:57–58

Appendix

Cling to God's Promises

Blessed

"A faithful man will abound with blessings, But he who makes haste to be rich will not go unpunished." (Proverbs 28:20)

"Blessed be the God and Father of our Lord Jesus Christ, who has blessed us with every spiritual blessing in the heavenly places in Christ." (Ephesians 1:3)

"Grace and peace be multiplied to you in the knowledge of God and of Jesus our Lord; seeing that His divine power has granted to us everything pertaining to life and godliness, through the true knowledge of Him who called us by His own glory and excellence." (2 Peter 1:2–3)

Also read 2 Samuel 7:18–29.

Encouragement (when you have been disobedient)

"For His anger is but for a moment, His favor is for a lifetime; Weeping may last for the night, But a shout of joy comes in the morning." (Psalm 30:5)

"He has not dealt with us according to our sins, Nor rewarded us according to our iniquities. For as high as the heavens are above the earth, So great is His lovingkindness toward those who fear Him. As far as the east is from the west, So far has He removed our transgressions from us." (Psalm 103:10–12)

"It is a trustworthy statement: For if we died with Him, we will also live with Him; If we endure, we will also reign with Him; If we deny Him, He also will deny us; If we are faithless, He remains faithful, for He cannot deny Himself." (2 Timothy 2:11–13)

"Therefore, since we have a great high priest who has passed through the heavens, Jesus the Son of God, let us hold fast our confession. For we do not have a high priest who cannot sympathize with our weaknesses, but One who has been tempted in all things as we are, yet without sin. Therefore let us draw near with confidence to the throne of grace, so that we may receive mercy and find grace to help in time of need." (Hebrews 4:14–16)

"My little children, I am writing these things to you so that you may not sin. And if anyone sins, we have an Advocate with the Father, Jesus Christ the righteous." (1 John 2:1)

Enemies

"The Lord will fight for you while you keep silent." (Exodus 14:14)

"That all this assembly may know that the Lord does not deliver by sword or by spear; for the battle is the Lord's and He will give you into our hands." (1 Samuel 17:47)

"Who is the King of glory? The Lord strong and mighty, the Lord mighty in battle." (Psalm 24:8)

"The Lord will protect you from all evil; He will keep your soul. The Lord will guard your going out and your coming in From this time forth and forever." (Psalm 121:7–8)

"You have enclosed me behind and before, and laid Your hand upon me." (Psalm 139:5)

"'No weapon that is formed against you will prosper; and every tongue that accuses you in judgment you will condemn. This is the heritage of the servants of the Lord, and their vindication is from Me,' declares the Lord." (Isaiah 54:17)

Also read Psalms 35 and 59.

Faithful

"God is not a man, that He should lie, nor a son of man, that He should repent; has He said, and will He not do it? Or has He spoken, and will He not make it good?" (Numbers 23:19)

"O Lord, You are my God; I will exalt You, I will give thanks to Your name; for You have worked wonders, plans formed long ago, with perfect faithfulness." (Isaiah 25:1)

"For I am confident of this very thing, that He who began a good work in you will perfect it until the day of Christ Jesus." (Philippians 1:6)

"Let us hold fast the confession of our hope without wavering, for He who promised is faithful." (Hebrews 10:23)

"The Lord is not slow about His promise, as some count slowness, but is patient toward you, not wishing for any to perish but for all to come to repentance." (2 Peter 3:9)

Fear

"Even though I walk through the valley of the shadow of death, I fear no evil, for You are with me; Your rod and Your staff, they comfort me." (Psalm 23:4)

"The Lord is my light and my salvation; whom shall I fear? The Lord is the defense of my life; whom shall I dread? When evildoers came upon me to devour my flesh, my adversaries and my enemies, they stumbled and fell. Though a host encamp against me, my heart will not fear; though war arise against me, in spite of this I shall be confident. One thing I have asked from the Lord, that I shall seek: that I may dwell in the house of the Lord all the days of my life, to behold the beauty of the Lord and to meditate in His temple. For in the day of trouble He will conceal me in His tabernacle; in the secret place of His tent He will hide me; He will lift me up on a rock." (Psalm 27:1–5)

"You, O Lord, will not withhold Your compassion from me; Your lovingkindness and Your truth will continually preserve me." (Psalm 40:11)

"You have taken account of my wanderings; put my tears in Your bottle. Are they not in Your book? Then my enemies will turn back in the day when I call; this I know, that God is for me. In God, whose word I praise, in the Lord, whose word I praise, in God I have put my trust, I shall not be afraid. What can man do to me? Your vows are binding upon me, O God; I will render thank offerings to You. For You have delivered my soul from death, indeed my feet from stumbling, so that I may walk before God in the light of the living." (Psalm 56:8–13)

"Do not fear, for I am with you; do not anxiously look about you, for I am your God. I will strengthen you, surely I will help you, surely I will uphold you with My righteous right hand." (Isaiah 41:10)

"For I am the Lord your God, who upholds your right hand, who says to you, 'Do not fear, I will help you.'" (Isaiah 41:13)

"But now, thus says the Lord, your Creator, O Jacob, and He who formed you, O Israel, "Do not fear, for I have redeemed you; I have called you by name; you are Mine! When you pass through the waters, I will be with you; and through the rivers, they will not overflow you. When you walk through the fire, you will not be scorched, nor will the flame burn you." (Isaiah 43:1–2)

"Then your light will break out like the dawn, and your recovery will speedily spring forth; and your righteousness will go before you; the glory of the Lord will be your rear guard." (Isaiah 58:8)

"'Do not be afraid of them, for I am with you to deliver you,' declares the Lord. ... 'They will fight against you, but they will not overcome you, for I am with you to deliver you,' declares the Lord." (Jeremiah 1:8–19)

Freedom

"'The Spirit of the Lord is upon me, because He anointed me to preach the gospel to the poor. He has sent me to proclaim release to the captives, and recovery of sight to the blind, to set free those who are oppressed.'" (Luke 4:18)

"So Jesus was saying to those Jews who had believed Him, 'If you continue in My word, then you are truly disciples of Mine; and you will know the truth, and the truth will make you free.' They answered Him, 'We are Abraham's descendants and have never yet been enslaved to anyone; how is it that You say, "You will become free?" Jesus answered them, "Truly, truly, I say to you, everyone who commits sin is the slave of sin."'" (John 8:31–34)

"But thanks be to God that though you were slaves of sin, you became obedient from the heart to that form of teaching to which you were committed, and having been freed from sin, you became slaves of righteousness. I am speaking in human terms because of the weakness of your flesh. For just as you presented your members as slaves to impurity and to lawlessness, resulting in further lawlessness, so now present your members as slaves to righteousness, resulting in sanctification. For when you were slaves of sin, you were free in regard to righteousness. Therefore what benefit were you then deriving from the things of which you are now ashamed?

For the outcome of those things is death. But now having been freed from sin and enslaved to God, you derive your benefit, resulting in sanctification, and the outcome, eternal life." (Romans 6:17–22)

"Now the Lord is the Spirit, and where the Spirit of the Lord is, there is liberty." (2 Corinthians 3:17)

Past, Present, and Future Hope

"For You formed my inward parts; You wove me in my mother's womb. I will give thanks to You, for I am fearfully and wonderfully made; Wonderful are Your works, And my soul knows it very well. My frame was not hidden from You, When I was made in secret, And skillfully wrought in the depths of the earth; Your eyes have seen my unformed substance; And in Your book were all written The days that were ordained for me, When as yet there was not one of them." (Psalm 139:13–16)

"'For I know the plans that I have for you,' declares the Lord, 'plans for welfare and not for calamity to give you a future and a hope.'" (Jeremiah 29:11)

"And although you were formerly alienated and hostile in mind, engaged in evil deeds, yet He has now reconciled you in His fleshly body through death, in order to present you before Him holy and blameless and beyond reproach–if indeed you continue in the faith firmly established and steadfast, and not moved away from the hope of the gospel that you have heard, which was proclaimed in all creation under heaven, and of which I, Paul, was made a minister." (Colossians 1:21–23)

"But we do not want you to be uninformed, brethren, about those who are asleep, so that you will not grieve as do the rest who have no hope. For if we believe that Jesus died and rose again, even so God will bring with Him those who have fallen asleep in Jesus. For this we say to you by the word of the Lord, that we who are alive and remain until the coming of the Lord, will not precede those who have fallen asleep. For the Lord Himself will descend from heaven with a shout, with the voice of the archangel and with the trumpet of God, and the dead in Christ will rise first. Then we who are alive and remain will be caught up together with them in the clouds to meet the Lord in the air, and so we shall always be with the Lord. Therefore comfort one another with these words." (1 Thessalonians 4:13–18)

"Let us rejoice and be glad and give the glory to Him, for the marriage of the Lamb has come and His bride has made herself ready." (Revelation 19:7)

Peace

"The steadfast of mind You will keep in perfect peace, because he trusts in You." (Isaiah 26:3)

"Do not let your heart be troubled; believe in God, believe also in Me." (John 14:1)

Appendix

"Peace I leave with you; My peace I give to you; not as the world gives do I give to you. Do not let your heart be troubled, nor let it be fearful." (John 14:27)

"Be anxious for nothing, but in everything by prayer and supplication with thanksgiving let your requests be made known to God. And the peace of God, which surpasses all comprehension, will guard your hearts and your minds in Christ Jesus. Finally, brethren, whatever is true, whatever is honorable, whatever is right, whatever is pure, whatever is lovely, whatever is of good repute, if there is any excellence and if anything worthy of praise, dwell on these things." (Philippians 4:6–8)

Prayer and Obedience

"If my people, which are called by my name, shall humble themselves, and pray, and seek my face, and turn from their wicked ways; then will I hear from heaven, and will forgive their sin, and will heal their land." (2 Chronicles 7:14)

"As for me, I shall call upon God, and the Lord will save me. Evening and morning and at noon, I will complain and murmur, and He will hear my voice." (Psalm 55:16–17)

"I cried to Him with my mouth, and He was extolled with my tongue. If I regard wickedness in my heart, the Lord will not hear; but certainly God has heard; He has given heed to the voice of my prayer. Blessed be God, who has not turned away my prayer nor His lovingkindness from me." (Psalm 66:17–20)

"The Lord is near to all who call upon Him, to all who call upon Him in truth. He will fulfill the desire of those who fear Him; He will also hear their cry and will save them." (Psalm 145:18–19)

"The Lord is far from the wicked, but He hears the prayer of the righteous." (Proverbs 15:29)

"Then you will call, and the Lord will answer; you will cry, and He will say, 'Here I am.' If you remove the yoke from your midst, the pointing of the finger and speaking wickedness." (Isaiah 58:9)

"Behold, the Lord's hand is not so short that it cannot save; nor is His ear so dull that it cannot hear. But your iniquities have made a separation between you and your God, and your sins have hidden His face from you so that He does not hear." (Isaiah 59:1–2)

"We know that God does not hear sinners; but if anyone is God-fearing and does His will, He hears him." (John 9:31)

"Whatever we ask we receive from Him, because we keep His commandments and do the things that are pleasing in His sight." (1 John 3:22)

"This is the confidence which we have before Him, that, if we ask anything according to His will, He hears us. And if we know that He hears us in whatever we ask, we know that we have the requests which we have asked from Him." (1 John 5:14–15)

Rejoicing Always

"You will make known to me the path of life; in Your presence is fullness of joy; in Your right hand there are pleasures forever." (Psalm 16:11)

"One thing I have asked from the Lord, that I shall seek: that I may dwell in the house of the Lord all the days of my life, to behold the beauty of the Lord and to meditate in His temple. For in the day of trouble He will conceal me in His tabernacle; in the secret place of His tent He will hide me; He will lift me up on a rock. And now my head will be lifted up above my enemies around me, and I will offer in His tent sacrifices with shouts of joy; I will sing, yes, I will sing praises to the Lord." (Psalm 27:4–6)

"I would have despaired unless I had believed that I would see the goodness of the Lord in the land of the living. Wait for the Lord; be strong and let your heart take courage; yes, wait for the Lord." (Psalm 27:13–14)

"I will bless the Lord at all times; His praise shall continually be in my mouth." (Psalm 34:1)

"For You have tried us, O God; You have refined us as silver is refined. You brought us into the net; You laid an oppressive burden upon our loins. You made men ride over our heads; we went through fire and through water, yet You brought us out into a place of abundance." (Psalm 66:10–12)

"These things I have spoken to you, so that in Me you may have peace. In the world you have tribulation, but take courage; I have overcome the world." (John 16:33)

"They took his advice; and after calling the apostles in, they flogged them and ordered them not to speak in the name of Jesus, and then released them. So they went on their way from the presence of the Council, rejoicing that they had been considered worthy to suffer shame for His name. And every day, in the temple and from house to house, they kept right on teaching and preaching Jesus as the Christ." (Acts 5:40–42)

"And not only this, but we also exult in our tribulations, knowing that tribulation brings about perseverance; and perseverance, proven character; and proven character, hope; and hope does not disappoint, because the love of God has been poured out within our hearts through the Holy Spirit who was given to us." (Romans 5:3–5)

"But we have this treasure in earthen vessels, so that the surpassing greatness of the power will be of God and not from ourselves; we are afflicted in every way, but not crushed; perplexed, but not despairing; persecuted, but not forsaken; struck down, but not destroyed; always carrying about in the body the dying of Jesus, so that the life of Jesus also may be manifested in our body." (2 Corinthians 4:7–10)

"Therefore we do not lose heart, but though our outer man is decaying, yet our inner man is being renewed day by day. For momentary, light affliction is producing for us an eternal weight of glory far beyond all comparison, while we look not at the things which are seen, but at the things which are not seen; for the things which are seen are temporal, but the things which are not seen are eternal." (2 Corinthians 4:16–18)

"Consider it all joy, my brethren, when you encounter various trials, knowing that the testing of your faith produces endurance. And let endurance have its perfect result, so that you may be perfect and complete, lacking in nothing." (James 1:2–4)

"Blessed is a man who perseveres under trial; for once he has been approved, he will receive the crown of life which the Lord has promised to those who love Him." (James 1:12)

"After you have suffered for a little while, the God of all grace, who called you to His eternal glory in Christ, will Himself perfect, confirm, strengthen and establish you." (1 Peter 5:10)

Stability

"Then Moses called to Joshua and said to him in the sight of all Israel, 'Be strong and courageous, for you shall go with this people into the land which the Lord has sworn to their fathers to give them, and you shall give it to them as an inheritance. The Lord is the one who goes ahead of you; He will be with you. He will not fail you or forsake you. Do not fear or be dismayed.'" (Deuteronomy 31:7–8)

"I have set the Lord continually before me; because He is at my right hand, I will not be shaken." (Psalm 16:8)

"Cast your burden upon the Lord and He will sustain you; He will never allow the righteous to be shaken." (Psalm 55:22)

"My soul, wait in silence for God only, for my hope is from Him. He only is my rock and my salvation, My stronghold; I shall not be shaken. On God my salvation and my glory rest; the rock of my strength, my refuge is in God. Trust in Him at all times, O people; Pour out your heart before Him; God is a refuge for us. Selah." (Psalm 62:5–8)

"Shadrach, Meshach and Abed-nego replied to the king, 'O Nebuchadnezzar, we do not need to give you an answer concerning this matter. If it be so, our God whom we serve is able to deliver us from the furnace of blazing fire; and He will deliver us out of your hand, O king. But even if He does not, let it be known to you, O king, that we are not going to serve your gods or worship the golden image that you have set up.'" (Daniel 3:16–18)

Strength

"Nevertheless I am continually with You; You have taken hold of my right hand. With Your counsel You will guide me, And afterward receive me to glory. Whom have I in heaven but You? And besides You, I desire nothing on earth. My flesh and my heart may fail, But God is the strength of my heart and my portion forever. For, behold, those who are far from You will perish; You have destroyed all those who are unfaithful to You. But as for me, the nearness of

God is my good; I have made the Lord GOD my refuge, That I may tell of all Your works." (Psalm 73:23–28)

"Do you not know? Have you not heard? The Everlasting God, the Lord, the Creator of the ends of the earth Does not become weary or tired. His understanding is inscrutable. He gives strength to the weary, And to him who lacks might He increases power. Though youths grow weary and tired, And vigorous young men stumble badly, Yet those who wait for the Lord Will gain new strength; They will mount up with wings like eagles, They will run and not get tired, They will walk and not become weary." (Isaiah 40:28–31)

"And He has said to me, 'My grace is sufficient for you, for power is perfected in weakness.' Most gladly, therefore, I will rather boast about my weaknesses, so that the power of Christ may dwell in me. Therefore I am well content with weaknesses, with insults, with distresses, with persecutions, with difficulties, for Christ's sake; for when I am weak, then I am strong." (2 Corinthians 12:9–10)

BIBLIOGRAPHY

Barna, George. *The Second Coming of the Church.* Nashville, Tennessee: Word Publishing, 1998.

Robertson, Archibald, Thomas. *Word Pictures in the New Testament.* Nashville, Tennessee: Broadman Press, 1981.

Strong, James. *The Exhaustive Concordance of the Bible:* (electronic ed.) Woodside Bible Fellowship. Ontario 1996.

Zodiathes, Spiros. *The Complete Word Study Old Testament.* Chattanooga, Tennessee: AMG Publishers, 1993.

Zodiathes, Spiros. *The Complete Word Study Dictionary: New Testament.* Chattanooga, Tennessee: AMG Publishers, 1992.

Zodiathes, Spiros. *The Complete Word Study New Testament.* Chattanooga, Tennessee. AMG Publishers, 1991.

Wilson, *William. Wilson's Old Testament Word Studies.* McLean, Va. MacDonald Publishers.

Books, CDs and Tapes
by J. Wilcoxson

Books

The "Word" on Health and Nutrition
Let Not Your Heart Be Troubled
Looking for Love in the Wrong Place
Thy Word: A Lamp unto my Feet

Tapes and CDs

- God Is
- Wait on the Lord
- Knowing God
- Jude (Studying Inductively)
- Rejoicing in Tribulation
- Faith: A Mother's Legacy
- Forgetting, Pressing, Reaching
- Living in the Power of His Resurrection
- Nutrition and Health
- Word Up: The Power of His Name

**For additional information
on tapes, CDs, videos, or books, contact:**

Sound Words
P. O. Box 2105
Dayton, OH 45401-2105
www.soundwords1.org

To order additional copies of

Let My PEOPLE GO

Have your credit card ready and call

Toll free: (877) 421-READ (7323)

or order online at: www.winepressbooks.com